Cultural Landscape Transaction and Values of Nupe Community in Central Nigeria

Isa Bala Muhammad

School of Environmental Technology,
Federal University of Technology, Minna, Nigeria

Vernon Series in Anthropology

VERNON PRESS

www.vernonpress.com

In the Americas:
Vernon Press
1000 N West Street,
Suite 1200, Wilmington,
Delaware 19801
United States

In the rest of the world:
Vernon Press
C/Sancti Espiritu 17,
Malaga, 29006
Spain

Vernon Series in Anthropology

Library of Congress Control Number: 2017948020

ISBN: 978-1-62273-285-2

To the memories of My Father, Alhaji Muhammad Nda-Isa

Foreword

Rural communities in Nigeria offer tremendous opportunities to study their cultural landscape, due to the existence of diverse ethnic groups and cultural settings. This is similar with communities throughout South-East Asia, particularly those of Indonesian settings. Cultural landscape in Nigeria is nurtured by transactions of the people with their surroundings that generate meaning and values. This book relates cultural values of the Nupe people, a minority ethnic group in North-central Nigeria, forming their cultural landscape that governs and sustain the communities' heritage.

Tangible building practices and varieties of crop production are among the functional performances signifying the identity of Nupe people and their communities. Besides, intangible values such as medicinal rituals and significance of the *gozan* (barber) aligned the people with their fellow villagers. These relationships provide insight on the natural and social settings traced to the family, which were revealed through an ethnography conducted by Dr Muhammad Isa Bala. For a period of eight (8) months he observed daily and seasonal practices of the Nupe community. Thereafter, he used illustrations to support assertions which are drawn out from the natives' perception of their cultural landscape in order to form his grounded theory. The grounded theory asserted that three (3) unique factors shaped a typical Nupe community; 1. The landscape– that include farms, greenery, hills and rivers, showcasing people-space and place relationship. 2. The architectural components– that include Katamba and Zhempa as typical domestic space shaped by family structure, and 3. The indigenous professions– that include *gozan* and the performance of *wasa*.

One of the significant achievements of Dr Muhammad's work is the devotion of the book on the intangible values (over the tangibles) of the Nupe cultural landscape and the promotion of the integration of these values in government policies. Indeed, a proposition that significantly aligns with UN's advocacy– on the consideration of mainstream social values in sustainable development goals of spatial implication. Also, Dr Muhammad's work consistently advocated for the preservation of values and identities of cultural landscapes.

Beyond these the greatest benefit derivable from studying Nupe cultural landscape is the unveiling of the socio-spatial interaction and relationships (myth and beliefs) of the Nupe ethnic group with their environment.

Ismail bin Said
Universiti Teknologi Malaysia

Table of Contents

List of tables

List of figures

Preface

Over time, values are culturally developed by people as they relate to the environment in both tangible and intangible forms. However, limited studies or documentations exist on cultural landscapes of minority ethnic groups, especially in developing nations. As such, there is a global call in which UNESCO is at the forefront advocating the need for the preservation of values and identities of cultural landscapes. The uniqueness of this book is on the empirical evidence based on the documentation of an eight-month ethnographic study of minority ethnic group in central Nigeria, the Nupes. One of the distinguishing characters of the cultural values of the Nupe people is that they have their cultural landscape transactions constituted in both tangible and intangible forms. Even though it relates to an ethnic group in central Nigeria, others from similar cultural landscape can relate to the cultural transactions discussed in different chapters of this book.

Readers can align to how cultural landscapes are expressed in both tangible and intangible forms. Equally important are the people-space and place relationship which results in a sense of place. The cultural values of communities are a product of both natural as well as the social setting which begins with the family. As such the Nupe basic family structure and its relationship with the domestic space are discussed in this book to give the reader an insight and also exemplify how cultural values are constituted within the domestic space.

Additionally, the economic lifestyle of people has an influence on the cultural landscape values of communities. Accordingly, a section of this book demonstrates this assertion as well as how cultural values are exhibited by indigenous professions in their transactions with the landscape. The concluding chapter of this book gives the deductions drawn from the cultural landscape values of Nupe community which resulted in the formulation of Grounded Theory with spatial implications.

It is to be noted that, the book is an edited PhD dissertation of the Author on cultural landscape of Nupe community in central Nigeria (Muhammad, 2015).

Acknowledgement

First, I would like to thank Professor Dr Ismail Said, for his tremendous effort, motivation, and untiring academic advice, especially on the initial research which formed the foundation for this book. My warmest appreciation goes to my family whose tolerance, support and prayers made it possible, they deserve to be mentioned. They are my wife Hajara, and my children, Fati, Munir, Nabil, Khalil, and Safira. In this category are also my Mother, Inna-Tako and my mother-in-law Mummy- (Habiba). I also appreciate the support my siblings namely; Yalarai, laminde, Umar, Bakar, Usman, Suleiman, Yusuf, Halimah and Yakubu. I am obligated to Dr AA Muhammad-Oumar for the valuable support before and also during the research process. The guidance, support and motivation of Mallam Kudu Liman and Dr Muhammad Ndatsu Mahmud are deeply appreciated.

My special appreciation goes to, Professor Ibrahim Kolo, Alhaji Manman Chado, Mallam Kudu Gona, they provided some vital information on the studied community. Similarly, in this class is the village head of Doko community, Alhaji Muhammad Dzhimau Santati as well as several respondents who are too numerous to mention. However, it is worth mentioning the names of some respondents, who passed away before the fruition of this book, they are Yawoba, Mr David Ndalangba, and Yababa Dokochi.

My appreciation goes to the Tertiary Education Trust Fund, Nigeria (TET-FUND) for fellowship granted to me during the PhD program at Universiti Teknologi Malaysia.

Alhamdulillah.

Biography of the Author

Isa Bala Muhammad obtained his PhD in Architecture from Universiti Teknologi Malaysia in 2015. He had his Master's Degree as well as bachelor's degree in architecture in 2000 and 2002 respectively from Federal University of Technology Minna. He joined the services of the Niger State government as an architect in 2003 where he designed and supervised several government projects and rose to the position of Architect I. Later on in 2007, he joined the Federal University of Technology Minna as a lecturer. He has written several articles on related subjects. His research interest is on, Ethnography, Cultural landscapes, Ecosystem Services and Human Behaviour and Environment

Chapter 1

Ethnography Approach to Cultural Landscape Studies

Introduction

Cultural Landscapes are made up of culture, environment, and the people. Each of the three components of the cultural landscape is filled with diverse and complex definitions. However, for this book, cultural landscape is operationalized to mean the social transactions and endless history of social transactions of people living within a community. It is the collective perspective and a way of living of the members of a given community (Palang *et al.*, 2011). As such, cultural landscape includes beliefs and cultural values constituted by people living within a community.

It, therefore, means that cultural landscape is the transactions of people with their landscape and the meaning and values people derive from such interactions (Lemelin *et al.*, 2015; Vejre *et al.*, 2010). These values are expressed in tangible and intangible forms depending on how people transact with their landscapes. Aside from culture, the socio-economic activities of the people contribute to how the landscapes are valued (Torquati *et al.*, 2015). For example, the socioeconomic activity of most rural African communities is farming; as such arable land becomes one of the key cultural value indicators for most communities.

Cultural landscapes are characterised by unique cultural transactions, but few studies exist, especially in the minority ethnic groups, (Nasongkhla, 2010). This is more profound on the African continent despite its richness in cultural heritage. For instance, Nigeria with a population of over 160 million people (NPC, 2006), and with over 250 ethnic groups has most cultural studies focused on the three ethnic groups of Hausa, Yoruba, and Igbo, (Adegbija, 2004). Each cultural transaction knowledge, as well as concepts, has a contributory role in extending knowledge beyond its geographical boundary. Furthermore, the importance of the Nupe ethnic group has seen it being noted amongst the fourteen communities celebrated by the Muslim reformer Sheik Usman fondue in the early 18th century (Musa, 2004; Sarki, 2010).

The importance of studies on minority ethnic group has continued to be in the forefront of intergovernmental organisations. For example, UNESCO's Director-General Bokova (2015) affirmed the importance indigenous values and such values and identities belong to all and must be protected by all.

However, each cultural landscape transactions are constituted differently and by extension expressed both in tangible and intangible forms. It, therefore, means that the understanding of cultural identities, especially those which are devoid of much research requires exploratory study (Glaser and Strauss, 2009). And for an exploratory study on people's perceptions, beliefs, and values, ethnography, therefore, becomes a good medium for the elicitation of information (Biklen, 2010).

Cultural landscape transactions are spatially constituted in different scales. The scale starts from the room, the compound, up to the entire community. However, the primary unit of social transactions in all cultural landscapes is the family unit (Martin, 2015). As such, it is important to include the family structure as well as their basic spatial transactions when cultural landscape values are studied. Furthermore, the boundary of spatial transactions is guided by the extent to which the daily needs of the family members are fulfilled.

Accordingly, it is to be established that the theoretical stance of this book is that, there exist a strong relationship between landscape character and the socio-cultural life of the people who occupy such landscapes (Cieraad, 2006). It also means that the occupation of the people influences how spaces are configured and also how transactions occur. Similarly, the elements of the cultural landscape transactions include both man-made and the natural landscape such as the streams, hills and vegetation. Consequently, the summation of all the foregoing thus leads to the understanding of the cultural landscape values of communities (Cullotta and Barbera, 2011; Stephenson, 2005; Zube and Pitt, 1981). On the whole, three factors constitute the bases for understanding cultural landscape transaction; they are the livelihood, family structure and the character of the domestic space as well as the landscape.

Tangible and intangible cultural values

Cultural landscape transactions are associated with physical and non-physical meaning. The landscape transaction also portrays the idiosyncrasy of a community and thus reflects the values of the people (del Barrio *et al.*, 2012). The concept of cultural values over time got expanded from the initial notion of monuments, historical buildings and archaeological site to also include the recognitions of people's collective identity. As a matter of fact, UNESCO at its various conventions emphasised the need to embrace the tangible and intangible elements of cultural heritage (Gullino and Larcher, 2012; Rössler, 2006; WHC, 1994). The advocacy thus became built up towards the inclusion of intangible cultural heritage, which was ignored for a long time, as a heritage to be protected and safeguarded (Vecco, 2010). Accordingly, UNESCO defined intangible cultural heritage to include people's processes, knowledge, skills, and products created as well social transactions with spaces. These socio-spatial processes which are mostly uniquely constituted in each culture provides a sense of continuity with the previous generations.

Contrastingly, within the context of developing nations such as Nigeria, little documentations exist on the concept and realities of preserving intangible values constituted in the landscape transactions of people and their cultural landscapes. This is not too different from what has been reported from South Africa (Muller, 2008). This suggests that the African continent needs to rise up to the challenge and recognition of the role of memory and meaning of place in its present form through the documentations of cultural landscape transactions and its values. It is to be noted, however, that, the documentation of the intangible cultural values is most at times represented not only in the physical forms but to also include the intangible forms. It, therefore, means that the understanding of cultural landscape transactions should be studied through the world view of the inhabitants. More also is that cultural values are constituted differently across cultures (Bergeron *et al.*, 2014)

Ethnography and cultural transactions

There exists an intimate connection between people and the world. To understand such connection, the basic principle is for the researcher to get immersed in the study of the phenomena (Seamon, 2000; Seamon and Sowers, 2008). The effectiveness of ethnography experience relies on getting involved as much as possible in the lives of the people. Ethnography effectiveness comes with the researcher assuming not to know the phenomena being studied and therefore the researcher is expected to be open to learning new phenomena (Nelson, 2011). Similarly, the researcher is also expected to be flexible in the elicitation of information since no two studies are the same. As such, a good ethnographic approach to cultural landscape studies is that which approaches human experiences in an unstructured, rich and in multi-dimensional ways. More also is that cultural landscapes are associated with multifaceted dimensions of views and interpretations.

Ethnographic approach in cultural landscape is associated with the interpretation of human experience and meanings as people carry out their daily routine. Ethnography, therefore, looks at the nature of environment and behaviour of people in an environment, but with the emphasis more on why such places are important to the people (Hermann, *et al.*, 2014). Similarly, ethnography seeks to describe the quality of the lived experience of people within an environment. Such lived experiences include what people see, hear, touch, smell and understand about their environment (van Manen and Adams, 2010). There exist, however, two approaches to people- place relationship inquiry. They are the idealist and the realist form of view to the study of the phenomenon. The idealist looks at the relationship of people with the environment as a conscious shaping of the world and assumes that people concretely know what they are doing. Here the assumption is that the environment has no effect on what people do in shaping their landscape. While the realist views people's place relationship as that in which the world acts on people and people react back (Mackenzie and Knipe, 2006). The two situations are, however, argued, because the perspectives of both the idealist and the realist looked at the environment and people as separate entities. However, a third-dimension asserts that people and environment act on each other holistically. This third dimension of people and the environment, forming a holistic entity is the inclination of this book. This is because of dual advantages; first, it leads to a better interpretation of man-made features and the reasons behind such creations. Secondly, human experiences which are exhibited in tangible and intangible forms contribute to environmental order through which senses of place are imbibed (Rippon, 2013). More also is that the third dimension is more alienable to ethnography which allows information about people's culture to be understood through their perception and world view.

Ethnographic approach to cultural landscape studies requires a lot of time to be spent with the people (Risjord, 2007). As such, for an effective ethnographic work, only one community can be studied at a time (O'Reilly, 2009). This is to allow an in-depth understanding of the cultural landscape transactions of the community. As such this work choose a rural Nupe community called Doko in central Nigeria. Hence, all references made to Nupe community are ascribed to only one case study, Doko community and not to the entire Nupeland. However, it is believed that many Nupe communities will draw inferences from this case study.

Chapter 2

The Meaning of Culture and Cultural Landscape

Defining culture and cultural landscape

Culture is constituted with a system which is made up of inherited symbols and objects used in communication and the generation of meaning between people (Linehan and Gross, 1998; Ujang and Zakariya, 2015). Culture is the view of people living within a particular community which differentiates them from another community (Woodside *et al.*, 2011). It also includes community's traditional ways of living, local wisdom, beliefs, and myths which get passed down from one generation to another (Price *et al.*, 2014). Various definitions are given on what culture entails, but what is common to all the definitions are that culture forms the basis of identity for a given group of people either in the belief system or the ways in which they carry out their activities.

Several perspectives exist in the definition of the cultural landscape. Van Eetvelde and Antrop (2009) For example, described cultural landscape to be any recognizable environment which is made up of individual entities of both living and non-living. As such, cultural landscapes constitute the transactions of people within a given community with natural, and man- made features through a long history of slow evolution and harmonious integration (Niţă *et al.*, 2015).

However, cultural landscape interests differ and it depends on the expertise of the assessor. This is because, it is associated with different disciplines such as geography (Cullotta and Barbera, 2011) archaeology (Bal *et al.*, 2015), landscape ecology (Hermann *et al.*, 2014; Turner *et al.*, 2014) and heritage (Zhang *et al.*, 2015). Aside from these disciplines, there also exist the social perspectives such as human psychology as seen in (Velarde *et al.*, 2007) and (Niţă, *et al.*, 2015). For this book, the cultural landscape is operationalized to mean the transactions of indigenous people with their landscape towards the fulfilment of their daily needs (Ujang and Zakariya, 2015). Equally important is that it also includes the meaning embedded within the transactions of people with their landscape and how such expressions are represented spatially (Anderson *et al.*, 2013). This rests on the premise that the transactions of indigenous people with their environment, creates a cultural identity (Antrop, 1997). More to this is that people develop values and meanings and identity over time. This identity could be from the natural features, man-made or even history related to the landscape. Cultural landscape, therefore, means nature and people, the past and the present, physical and social attributes all subsumed into one (Muhammad and Said, 2015b). To rephrase, cultural landscape means the relationship of nature and man within a given geographical location (Bokova, 2015; Rössler, 2006).

The interest of studies in the relationship between people and nature, over time, has gained prominence. Some of the attributes associated with cultural landscapes are the meaning and values indigenous people drive from their environment. In fact, (ELC, 2012) resolution stated that amongst other criteria to be included in the choice of heritage sites is people's identity as expressed in their landscape, both in tangible and intangible forms (Gullino and Larcher, 2012). In the same perspective, the European Landscape convention (Jones, 2007) acknowledges that cultural landscapes play an important role in contributing to human well-being and identity. By and large, the study of cultural landscapes can never be over emphasised, more also is that it allows for the development of People versus landscape transaction policies (Donovan and Gkartzios, 2014).

Cultural landscape values assessment

A plethora of fields of study can be seen to apply landscape assessment. Some of the common methods of assessment of landscape are the quality assessment (Ramírez et al., 2011), ecological assessment (Tian et al., 2014), and cultural heritage assessment (Gullino and Larcher, 2012). Landscape quality assessments are mostly carried out by landscape architects such that quality is perceived in the realms of the visual or experiential qualities of the landscape. Thus, the assessment is inclined towards picturesque principles. While for the ecologist, the assessment of landscape is premised on the ecological importance of the various parts of the landscape such as its naturalness and the degree of human interference. These types of assessment are generally carried in a localised environment such as a pond, which may look at the effect of inorganic substances on the species of fish in the pond (Ódor et al., 2014).

Similarly, assessment of landscape values can also be on the heritage protection movement which advocates for the need to preserve antiquities and monuments such as historical buildings. Protection of buildings and historic settings where the initial concept through which people's values about their landscape were concentrated upon. Later on, concerns began to emerge on the associative values of spaces. The associative values of the landscape are linked to several factors some of which are culture, the nature of the landscape and the type of economic activity that takes place in the community. It is in these transactions that, people also confer meanings and values (Bergeron, et al., 2014). The meaning and values could be tangible and intangible (Nunta and Sahachaisaeree, 2010). For example, a particular tree could provide a tangible benefit of fruit and shade for a particular locality while in another community its value could be for spiritual benefits (Gunner, 2005). This suggests that a universal template for measurement of the cultural landscape is nearly impossible especially when such assessment is to be carried out through the perspective of a non-native person. It, therefore, means that the assessment of cultural landscape values requires an insider's perspective. By an insider perspective, it means understanding native people's world view about their landscape (Stephenson, 2008). This is because values are culturally defined and therefore differences exist on what society holds tightly and what they do not (Stolley, 2005).

Cultural values are constituted in different forms more also is that people do not act towards the physical landscape alone, but also on its intangible cultural meaning. The physical landscape is available for the assessor to decipher, but the meaning which is not necessarily a material object is not. Thus, the more appropriate means of cultural landscape assessment is that which is carried out through the worldview of the indigenous people living within the landscape. More also is that values of the landscape are constituted in tangible and the intangible form (Anderson, et al., 2013).

The tangible value of the landscape is centred on the physicality of the landscape which is understood both by the insider and the visitor (Stephenson, 2008). While the intangible value of the landscape is associated with meanings which are concealed such that it is the residents of such landscape that appreciate such type of values (Bergeron, et al., 2014; Tengberg et al., 2012). Similarly, the intangible values of landscapes are also related to the memories and lived experiences which are mostly ingrained within the people who reside within a given landscape.

It is to be noted, however, that the tangible and intangible values of the landscape are inseparable. This is because the intangible value of the landscape is materialised by the tangible feature of the landscape. In other words, intangible values of the landscape would not manifest without the tangible features of the landscape. In general, Peoples, perceptions, meanings, social procedures and the traditions contribute to the intangible values of the landscape. This is to say that, the cultural landscape values assessment also requires the understanding of the history of the indigenous people's past as well as the activities of the present. In other words, the stories and history of the community offer a holistic understanding of landscape values of communities (Taylor, 2008) and also socio-cultural connections of the past and the present (House, 2010). Markedly, memories of the past become a common rallying point within a social group which also forms part of the cultural identity (Wheeler, 2014).

These imply that the manifestations of intangible cultural landscape values are found in memories associated with the physical landscape (Drozdzewski, 2014). Furthermore, cultural landscapes are not concealed in perceptions alone, nor do they exist solely on the physical features, but also includes the human relationship with the environment and the cognitive meaning and values attributed to the landscape, (Seamon, 2015). It is also to be noted that cultural landscape values are constituted in different forms; hence the values are laid on what is found meaningful and also treasured by the indigenous people. Above all, it is about the meaning and values that space and place are constituted (Parsaee et al., 2014).

Space and sense of place

The social connections of people are grounded in space. This is to say that people's transactions occur in a physically defined area which carries meaning with it. When such meaning is developed, it transcends from being a space to become a place (Róin, 2015). A place is therefore created based on people's experience of a given space. The creation of a place starts with the basic unit of spatial transaction; the domestic space. This is because; the domestic space serves as the primary base for social relationships of families (Coontz, 2000).

Despite all these, people's transactions are shaped by their social group, the type of family, and the community as a whole (Stolley, 2005). Opinions differ on what aspect of culture influences the use of space. However, people's influence in the use of space is affected by their cultural worldviews, values, and lifestyles. Spaces are therefore made to suit the socio-cultural life of people (Maina, 2013). This shows that people sharing a cultural tradition are also likely to share the same socio-spatial traits. It, therefore, means that within the domestic space, it is expected that certain traits of spatial behaviour of a culture would be the same. This thus showcases the use of space to be a reflection of culture which in turns influences architecture. For example, it is a natural human tendency to segment or partition an undifferentiated continuous space due to cultural requirements (Kent, 1993; Prussin, 1974). In line with this natural instinct, segmentations are bound to reflect in the indigenous architecture of the people. For example, in the Hausa community of northern Nigeria, where *kulle* or purdah (wife's seclusion) is practiced, a reflection of such cultural practice is seen in the traditional architecture where physical barriers are created between male and females (Muhammad-Oumar, 1997). Similarly, social transactions within domestic space across many cultures are gender specific (Pellow, 2003). The reason for this may not be farfetched because most transactions within the house are inclined towards women's activities such as domestic chores and caring for children.

Furthermore, there exist several factors that have effect on the social relationship of people within the domestic space. Rapoport (1993) describes these factors as a system of activities. They include the nature of activities that are being carried out, the relationship of such activities within the system and what such activities mean to the people. It, therefore, means that an activity system is tied to the sequence of the activity, the performer of such activity, where, when and also who is involved in the activity and why (Parsaee, *et al.*, 2014). Furthermore, the complete overview of domestic space transaction requires that each member of the family quotidian use of domestic space is taken into account. Amid these spatial transactions are also time-space routines of each member of the family (Muhammad and Said, 2015b). Time-space routines are the habitual bodily behaviours of people within a given environment. It is termed time-space routine because people are habitually found performing activities at a particular space and time. In addition, the time-based routines are culture-specific and therefore it contributes to defining the people- place relationship.

Similarly, as described by Howley *et al.*, (2012), the aesthetic of any given landscape are a function of the experience, behaviours, and relationship of people with the environment. Even though there are different stances on the aesthetics of the landscape, the foregoing gives the cue for the theoretical framework for this book. The framework lies within the symbolic interactionism which believes that each society is created through the daily transactions of people among themselves as well as the environment. More also is that it is under this circumstance that the life world experiences and tacit unnoticed knowledge are understood (Seamon, 2015).

Nupe community cultural landscape

Nupe communities are located in the middle region of Nigeria and they are situated within the lower basin of river Niger and Kaduna (Figure 2.1).

Substantial numbers of Nupe communities are found in Niger state with a spill into the neighbouring states of Kwara and Kogi. The most noticeable natural landscape feature is river Niger which cuts across Nupe communities as illustrated in Figure 2.2.

Furthermore, Nupe settlements are also found characterised with flat as well as hilly landscape as illustrated in Figure 2.3 and 2.4.

Figure 2.1: The Location of Nupeland in Central Nigeria

Figure 2.2: Dutsu, a rural Nupe community settlement along River Niger

Figure 2.3: Doko, a Nupe Community surrounded by a hilly landscape

Figure 2.4: The plain Landscape character allows for the cultivation of rice and other cereals for this Nupe community, Doko.

The landscape types and occupation have distinctively been used by the Nupes to identify themselves. Those living on the river banks and whose occupation is primarily fishing are regarded as the *Kyadya*. The non-riverine communities refer to themselves as *Kintsozhi*, the land, people (Nadel, 1942).

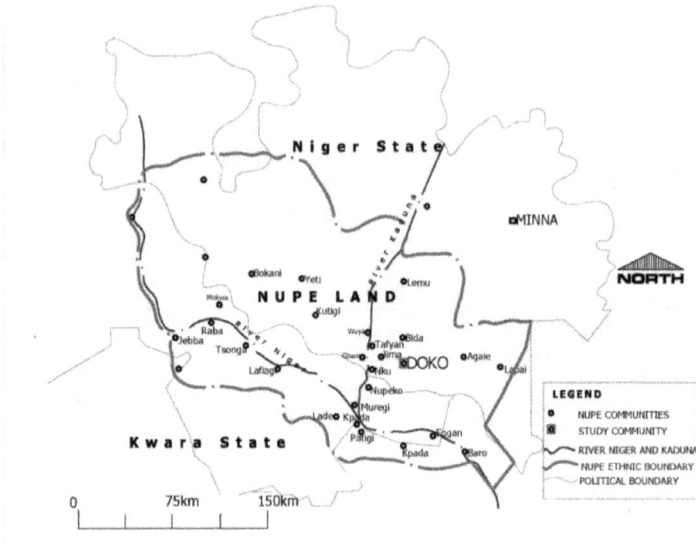

Figure 2.4: Nupe settlements along river Niger and Kaduna and those located on the upland

As such the ecological landscape of the Nupe communities offers a very wide range of economic resources of transportation and productions of different varieties of food crops. The Nupe have been known to live as a community since the early 13th and 14th century and they have been known to have a well-defined culture (Sarki, 2010). Such unique character of the Nupes is also seen in their conceptualisation of the family unit and by extension the conduct of marriage.

Situating marriage ceremony in Nupe community transactions

Marriage, especially in Africa, constitutes one of the fundamental bonds associated with a family organization (Draper, 1989). African landscape is made up of a complex institution of rituals and stage performance in the conduct of marriage (Meekers, 1992). As such, several cultural factors influence the conduct of marriage in Nupe communities. The influence is in two dimensions. First, the conduct of marriage requires financial inputs and thus farming as a primary profession in the community serves as the main source. Secondly, the Nupe community behavioural pattern of farming provides no room for the interjection of marriage ceremonies because it will break the rhythm of farming activities. Therefore, marriage ceremonies are conducted after the harvest of crops which is also a resting period for the locals. Furthermore, the festivities of marriage are conducted in an outdoors and thus the end of cropping season affords the local people the use of the outdoor space without the interference of the rain. The outdoor space, therefore, serves as an intangible space within the Nupe community cultural landscape.

It is worthy of mentioning that marriages in Nupe communities are period specific and thus occur during the dry season after the harvest of crops. Festivities of marriage are therefore more during the months of November to January before the start of the farming season. The Nupe people's transactions are therefore choreographed towards the incorporation of their culture, farming, social needs and climatic conditions of their landscape towards the fulfilment social needs which in this case is marriage.

Chapter 3

Family Structure and Domestic Space Transactions

Doko community landscape character

Doko town belongs to the Beni group[1] of Nupes and they are located in the upland which is surrounded by an outcrop of hill running from the southwest region to the northwest region of the community. The town was formed from the conglomeration of several clans who settled on the hill for protection against the early 18 century raids on Nupe communities. The hill as shown in Figure 3.1 is a dominant feature in the community landscape.

Figure 3.1: The hill surrounding Doko community landscape

---

[1] Beni Nupes are made up of twelve towns in a form of confederacy. The bond of confederacy was established towards the protection of one another during the period of inter-tribal wars in the early 18th century. For an extended history see (Nadel 1942).

Doko like most rural communities in Nigeria is predominantly farmers. The major crops cultivated are millet, corn, cassava and sweet potatoes on the uplands. While on the flood plains which is situated far away from the immediate vicinity of the settlement is used for the cultivation of rice. The community has all year-round agricultural related activities.

It is common and also long established that African rural communities live in an extended family system (Aldous, 1962). Similarly, such is also found in most Nupe communities (Muhammad and Said, 2015a). However, one striking observation of the family system is that some are not established purely on biological lineage. For example, in the Nupe community of Doko, it is a common norm for family head, *Ndamitso*, to adopt children from friends and also distant relatives. These adoptions could stem from the death of the children's parents, support for the weaker family or purely towards the enrichment of friendship ties and bond. The adopted children are thus engaged in the full occupation of the new family which is mostly farming. Markedly, farming forms the basis for the establishment of the Nupe family system called *efako*. *Efako* literally means a large piece of lands jointly worked on for farming by household members. As such, in the cultural landscape of Doko community all members, especially males who are under the care of a family head and also working on the same farm for the benefit of the family are referred to belong to the same *Efako*. The Nupe family, therefore, is established more on *Efako* than the blood relationship. This family structure system of living is buttressed by the quotation of a respondent below:

"dangi ga yiyo ebona efako nini gabo yi dao"

Which literally means; we are family because we are bonded through the cultivation of the same farm.

Dangi means related as well as family (Yisa, 2013). Therefore, the *Efako* formed the link of relationship which is not necessarily biological. As an illustration, Figure 3.2 is an outline of a structure of a family established based on the *efako* family system.

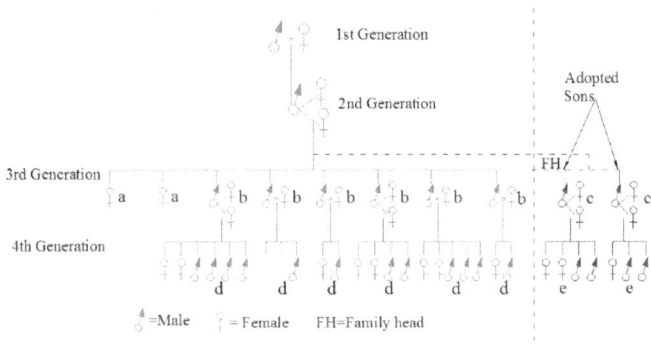

Figure 3.2: A four generation family structure diagram of the Nupe community

The establishment of the family stems from a husband and a wife who later begot only a male child. The son married two wives and had two biological females, six biological male children, and two adopted male children into the *Efako*. This formed the establishment of the 3rd generation of the family structure. Culturally, adoption of children is carried out based on different reasons. There are those made to increase the social bond between friends or families and those made out of the necessity of children being orphaned. In another instance, children are taken to seek for spiritual care and thence they become part of the *efako* (family). This is stipulated by respondent aged 55 in the following statement:

> *"The compound as you can see was established by Babandawodi who happens to be our great-grandfather, He was a powerful man and a very good medicine man and therefore children were brought to him for medical care and a lot joined his efako"*

The quotation shows how boys were taken to a family for adoption based on the family head's expertise as a traditional medicine and care giving to the weak in the community. What is to be noted is that once an adoption is made, the adopted child becomes a complete member of the family with the same rights with all other biological children of the family head. However, instances arise where the adopted children sought to go back to their roots, and in such situation, they lose the benefits and rights in the *efako*. As such, the development of a space and residency within the compound forms a strong condition for an adopted child to belong to an *efako*. If a child chooses to stay, the *efako* system allows for the transfer of equal patrilineal rights to the adopted child. For example, the leadership of compounds goes to the eldest male child. The eldest child in this instance can be either a biological or a non-biological son of the family head. This is exemplified in a family as illustrated in Figure 3.2

which shows the family head in the third generation to be an adopted son (FH). In this example, the family head (the adopted son) is given the full responsibility for the wellbeing and representation of the family in the village council. It is, however, worth mentioning that the *efako* family structure is inclined towards male members, especially in terms of leadership of the compound. Furthermore, the female members mostly do not inherit land properties as they are considered as members of another family through marriage. This can be deduced from this common saying in Nupe communities.

"Danan yan yizagi se emi eba"

The quotation means the place of a woman is in her spouse's house. This is the cultural norm and thus it has some spatial implications. Most important is that the provision of space and accommodation are more inclined to the male folk and therefore the females are accommodated in their mother's room up to the time they get married. However, one interesting implication of this is that it is a cultural prerequisite for the bridegroom to have at least a room built for the bride before marriage is conducted. As such, while women are most at times exempted from the inheritance of space and built up properties within their paternal homes, the groom will have to build at least a room for the bride before marriage is conducted. Furthermore, the womenfolk are financially supported by the male kit and kin right from the childhood stage up to the adulthood. For example, during marriage ceremonies the proceeds from the farming activities, a male domain is used in the conduct of the marriage purchase of cooking utensils and furniture. It is worth mentioning that the women utensils constitute a major cultural value in Nupe community.

The Nupe Women's Utensils and Spatial Transactions

The function of spaces such as the bedroom is enhanced by its furniture. One of the dominant furniture in a typical Nupe woman's room is the earthen pots. Earthen pots have historically been one of the first indicators of human inventions, especially in its function as domestic containers and wares. Likewise, the Nupe woman's bedroom is incomplete without the pots stacked up together as part of the furniture in the rooms as illustrated in Figure 3.3.

Furthermore, pots aside from their aesthetic functions, they are also used as storage wares within the courtyards, (see Figure 3.4).

Figure 3.3: A Nupe Woman's room decorated with pots.

Figure 3.4: Clay pots placed outside the courtyard for the storage of water and other wares.

It is not all Nupe communities that make pots, and as such most communities like Doko, rely on the neighbouring communities for the supply. For Doko community, pots were purchased from Patigi and Ebuagi communities which are about 25 kilometres away from the community. This can be considered as a long distance, especially during the period when the foot happened to be the main means of transportation. However, its significance and value in the lives of the women made it a worthwhile journey. This is further buttressed in the following anecdote by 85 years old Nupe Woman.

> *"My mum bought beautiful pots for me in which I decorated my room with. There were eight rows and each row had 4 pots. I had to sell 2 rows when I needed money"*

Aside from the aesthetic functions of pots, they also served as valuable assets which easily can be liquidated for money when the need arises. Furthermore, pots also constitute an element of pride to the Nupe women. This is expressed in the anecdote from the same respondent as follows:

> *"The only things left out of the gifts from my marriage are these pots, they are over 60 years old now, I cherish them"*

Aside from these, the Nupe woman transactions with pots is such that they are arranged systematically. The arrangement is made such that the larger pots are placed first and the smaller ones placed on top of each so that the smallest becomes the last pot on top.

Pots in the daily life of the local woman serve as a storage space; it is such that private items or valuables are stored in them away from the public view. It, therefore, means that the local women always have to transact with the pots almost on a daily basis because items such as grains and other valuables are kept inside them. These daily transactions are explained by a 65-year-old woman as follows:

> *"The wares I use every day are kept inside the topmost pots while those that are used less frequently are kept at the bottom"*

This may seem strenuous. However, the local woman goes about such storage systematically. Notably, this, therefore, constitutes an adaptive and cultural creativity associated with the use of pots in the typical local woman's room. It is such that the most frequently used wares are kept in the topmost pots. In doing so, the numbers of pots that are required to be displaced frequently is minimised. While on the other hand the less frequently used wares as well as valuable item such as jewellery are kept in the bottommost pots.

The advantage of doing this is that it takes a thief more time to get access to the items.

However, over time the decoration of bedrooms with pots has declined with the infiltration of other cultures and modernization. Nevertheless, the concept associated with the use of pots as decorative features, and storage space is beginning to be constituted in a different form as shown in Figure 3.5.

Figure 3.5: The concept of pot decoration replaced with enamelled wares

The pots are now being replaced with enamel steel wares, especially by the young women. However, the principle and the functions which the pots serve are transferred to the enamel wares. Pots, therefore, have different cultural values within the life and culture of the typical woman in the community. The transformation in the replacement of pots with enamelled wares still shows that the cultural concept upon which the use of pots was initiated in the first place is still maintained. Summarily, the highlight of this section showcases that cultural landscape transactions of the Nupe community which are tangibly and intangibly constituted with both having spatial implications.

Compound leadership and spatial implication

Compounds are divided into small family units through the formation of courtyards locally called *zhempa*. The family head, *emitso* in every nupe compound takes custody of the *katamba* entrance hut. As the leader of the compound, the *katamba* is where visitors are received during the ceremonies such as weddings, naming ceremonies and mourning. As such, each individual compound which is made up of several courtyards has at least one *katamba*. As an illustration, Figure 3.6 shows the location of the entrance hut *katamba*, and also the various courtyards representing each of the individual family units.

The *katamba* symbolically serves as an entry point into the compound which leads directly into the first courtyard. Most at times, as illustrated in Figure 3.6, the first courtyard of the Nupe compounds gives an indication of *Asali*. Courtyards are established for each nucleus family and therefore the number of courtyards gives an indication of the number of nucleus families within a compound. However, as the population outgrows the space available for expansion, the courtyard establishment stops. The saturation of available space within the ancestral home for further development leads to the reconstruction of the already built structures.

In Nupe communities, there exists a strong sense of attachment to their ancestral compounds. Most members of the family would keep on reconstructing the spaces to accommodate more rooms until it becomes impossible to do so. When the stage of saturation for expansion is reached, new compounds are established as close as possible to the ancestral home. This assertion is affirmed by a female respondent aged 55, in the following quotation:

> *"My brother bought the piece of land over there for his children as you can see, the main compound is filled up but the new compound is not too far from this house."*

This indicates the sense of connection and attachment of the Nupe people to their ancestral homes. Such closeness is also linked to the need to be near the *emitso*, the family head. This is because the *emitso* serve as the connection to the leadership of the community. Furthermore, staying within the ancestral home is what entitles a person to the leadership of the family.

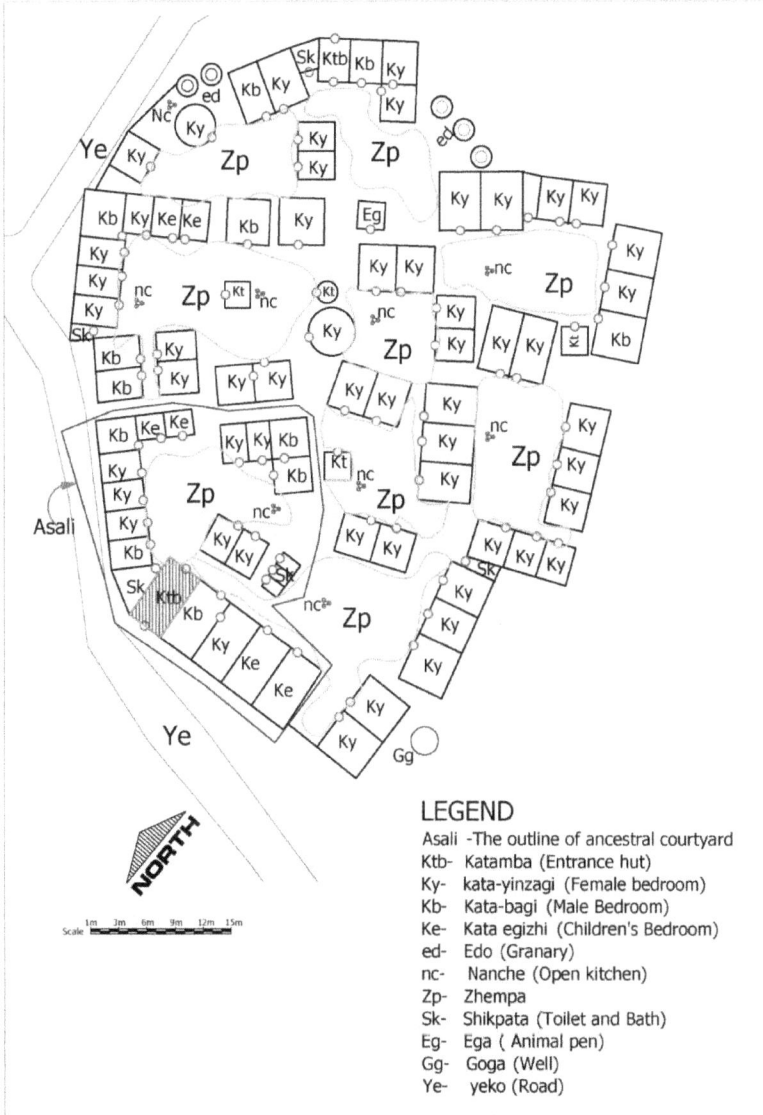

LEGEND

Asali - The outline of ancestral courtyard
Ktb- Katamba (Entrance hut)
Ky- kata-yinzagi (Female bedroom)
Kb- Kata-bagi (Male Bedroom)
Ke- Kata egizhi (Children's Bedroom)
ed- Edo (Granary)
nc- Nanche (Open kitchen)
Zp- Zhempa
Sk- Shikpata (Toilet and Bath)
Eg- Ega (Animal pen)
Gg- Goga (Well)
Ye- yeko (Road)

Figure 3.6: A typical compound made up a common entrance hut (*katamba*) with several individual courtyards

Most Nupe compounds can be found to have reached their climax of development as there is no more space for new structures. However, the male members of the family always ensure they have at least a room within the ancestral compound referred to as *asali*. This is because; ancestral compounds serve as a sense of pride to the community members. As such, it is not uncommon to find large buildings being demolished and reconstructed to give room for more smaller rooms. This is further explained by a female respondent age 45 in this quotation:

"My brother demolished our mother's circular room and rebuilt it to have three rooms"

The spatial implication sense of attachment to the ancestral home has seen a gradual decline in the number of the circular rooms to rectangularly shaped rooms. This is because it allowed for more rooms to be built. A compound as described by a family head on the location of circular rooms that were demolished and the new structure built in the spaces is illustrated in Figure 3.7

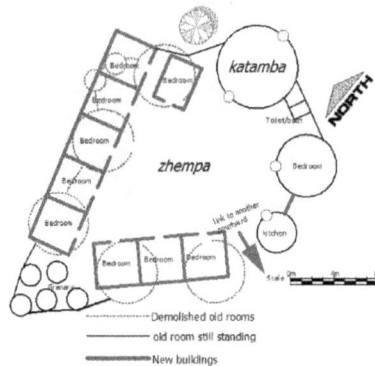

Figure 3.7: A layout showing change from circular to square shaped bedrooms

The layout (Figure 3.7) shows the original space occupied by five circular rooms occupying a space of 120 square meters, which over time got converted to occupy nine square bedrooms. It can also be noticed that the circular rooms were originally detached from one another. However, the squared shaped rooms were built attached to allow for more rooms. Despite the need for more rooms, the courtyard spaces were seen not tampered with, rather the area of the rooms are reduced from an average of 24 meters squared circular rooms to an average of 16 meters squared rectangular bedroom.

A typical Nupe person believes that ancestral homes are laden with the blessings of the founding fathers. Thus, to the Nupe people, it is important that they continue to receive the blessings of their forefathers who established the compound. As such, even new compounds, established outside the *asali* due to non-availability of space, does see such families move back to the *asali* compounds for ceremonies. An excerpt of the conduct of prayers as observed showcases an additional dimension of the sense of attachment of the Nupes to the ancestral homes.

> *"May Allah bless the child, may the blessings of the founding fathers of this compound be upon him, and may he be a blessing to the family, the compound and the entire community at large"*

These are the words of a Muslim cleric, offered on the naming of a child in an *asali* compound. If the prayers were conducted in a newly established compound, the direct reference to the founding fathers of the compound would not have been possible. Even though it can be argued that such reference to the forefathers could still be made symbolically anywhere, the physical presence in the ancestral compound is also important to the local people.

To rephrase, the Nupes do have a strong sense of attachment to their respective ancestral home so much so that they repartition spaces so as to have space in the ancestral home no matter how small it turns out to be.

Nupe domestic space transactions

The transactions of people within the domestic space are a function of how activities are carried out, the relationship of the activity with other activities, and the meaning people associate with such activities. Similarly, in such transactions, three categories of elements are involved; they are the fixed features the semi-fixed features and the people who utilise the space (Kent, 1993). In a typical compound of the Nupe community, the fixed features within a typical compound are the, entrance hut (*katamba*), sleeping rooms (*kata*), the courtyard, (*zhempa)*, the animal pen (*ega,*) the granaries (*edo*), the kitchen (*katagi*), the heart (*yekun)* and the toilets and baths (*shikpata*). A typical example of the compound layout of the Nupes has already been illustrated in Figure 3.6. Typically, fixed features (architecture) within a domestic space are important in the daily transactions of people, however, some spaces are more important in the functioning of the system (Hillier *et al.*, 1987). The determination of these spaces in order of importance and functioning of the system is made through observation of the frequency of people's interaction with such spaces. For example, Figure 3.8 is an analysis output of the frequency of spatial transactions of Nupes within the domestic space.

ARCHITECTURE

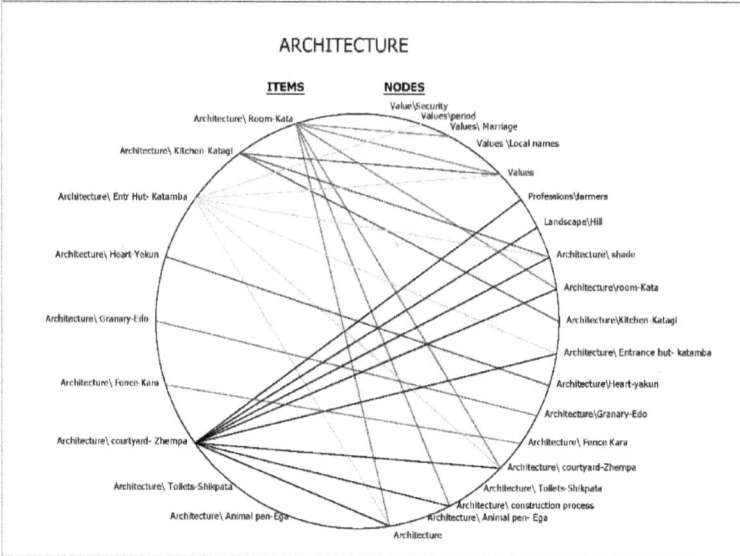

Figure 3.8: The Transactions connectivity map of domestic spaces

The connection map shows that *zhempa* (courtyard) has the highest connections of 8 strings which depicts the importance of the Nupe family's relationship with the courtyard (Muhammad and Said, 2015b). This is followed by
katamba and *kata* each having 6 connections respectively, while the *katagi*
has a 3-string connection. In essence, this shows that the importance of a
space is a function of the frequency of transactions of people with space as
well as the interrelation between one space to another space (Glaser and
Strauss, 2009). Thus, the most important domestic spaces of transactions in a
typical Nupe compound are *zhempa*, (courtyard) *kata* (bedroom) *katamba*
(entrance hall) and *katagi* (the kitchen). As such these four spaces will be the
subject of more elaborations on how a typical nupe family transacts with
these spaces. The discussions are focused on the children, the adult male, and
female. This is because these categories of people are adequate to represent
all transactions that are likely to occur within the domestic space.

Spatial transactions of children

The early socialization of the children in Nupe community is not limited to
the nuclear family, but also includes the extended family. This is because the
daily routine of children goes beyond the primary courtyard of their parents
and extends to all the courtyards within the compound. Part of the daily routine of children every morning is for them to go around and greet all the elders
of the extended family. This routine of morning greetings is spatially en-

hanced through *dzungi,* (connecting alleys) linking courtyards together. As the children grow older this social routine enables them to know the categories of people within the extended family structure such as uncles, cousins, and nephews. As such the child accords them the required respect for their status. Furthermore, the spatial connections of all the courtyards give a semblance of oneness and the child grows to know that the territory of relationship is not limited to his immediate family.

As such in Nupe community, children are all raised such that the extended family members do join in the moulding of the child in both character and skills. A respondent while discussing the attributes of respect as enshrined in the culture of the community mentioned: *"Eyeladan egi wun ji etun eza nini a"* which means raising children is a collective effort of the parent and the society.

This tradition is practiced in such a way that uncles, aunts, and cousins contribute their quarter in ensuring that the children follow and respect the ideal of the compound and the community as a whole. As such the fluidity of the compound layout in which all courtyards are linked affords social connections between the elders within the family and children. The fluidity and connections of courtyards create the opportunity and a larger spatial area within the extended family compound for children to play. Again, collectively all children are also found to assemble at either the back of the house or the front under the shade of a tree to play (Figure 3.9 and 3.10).

The cultural landscape affords the children the material for play. As illustrated in Figure 3.10, the material of the play is the corn stalks, a product of the farm produce. Furthermore, in such plays, the children are seen constructing spaces to represent room, toilets, and alleys. This is mimicry of what they see adults do in construction. A discussion with one of the children age 6, on their creation, is noted below:

"We constructed two rooms, Katamba, and a toilet"

What is deduced from this narration is that the children gave a reflection of important architectural spaces. They ensured that the *katamba,* (the entrance hall) kata (the room) and the *shikpata* (toilet) are represented, while the kitchen, the granary, and other spaces are left out. It is to be noted that in this scenario of children's play, an important feature is left out in the conception of the children's architecture. The reason for this could either be the limitation of the children's ability to represent such space or it could be that it does not constitute an important space for the children when compared to the bedrooms and the front of the compound where children are always found to play. What is important is that even within the subconsciousness of children, they are able to conceptualise in concrete form the spaces that matter to them.

Figure 3.9: Children, about the age of 2 to 4 years playing under a tree in front of a compound

Figure 3.10: Children age 4 to 6 playing under the tree with corn stalk in front of a compound

Similarly, it is also common to find children extending their play from the vicinity of the compound to the fields. For example, children within the cultural landscape are found to use hunting as a form of play some distance away from the community as depicted in Figure 3.11.

Figure 3.11: Children studying the tracks left by rodents

Hunting within the community is taken as a leisure activity, especially after the harvest of crops which occurs between November and December every year. During this period the youths are seen to go into the wider landscape several kilometres away from the community. A discussion with one respondent, age 16, stated the following:

> *"Five of us left the community after the break of the dawn and got back after the call of second-day prayer, I came back with a rabbit."*

Youths within the cultural landscape engage themselves during the dry season, which lapses between Januarys and March. Undoubtedly, the hunting activity of the youths serves as a template of mimicry for the children. However, the children's territory is limited to the immediate vicinity of the compound. Other transactions of children also include such activities which include taking food to their parents on the farm and going to the evening market for the family supplies. Children could cover a distance of a few meters up to one kilometre on an errand. Children are thus found equally engaged in both internal activities within the compound as well as external activities outside the compound.

Zhempa (courtyard) and family transaction

Zhempa in the cultural landscape refers to as an exterior out of the door space within the enclave of an occupied house. *Zhempa* is mostly irregular in shape, but closer to a circular formation with different types of rooms forming the external circumference. A typical *zhempa* is surrounded by at least a kitchen, animal pen, and bedrooms. It is a space that provides for the drying of clothes, placement of earthen pots for storage of water and drying of farm products. It is a place that women utilised for routine domestic chores and as such, the courtyards is a women's territory. This is because, during the day, the men leave the house for their farms and on their return in the evenings, the front of the house near the *katamba* (the entrance hut) serves as the resting place.

The dawn marks the beginning of the day for most families and the first point of call is the courtyard. It is a space where breakfast is prepared and also taken by both male and female members of the family. At the end of breakfast, the men leave for their farms while the women folk are left to carry on their domestic chores. Domestic chores of a typical Nupe woman include fetching water from the well and storage into the earthen pots found within the courtyards. Other activities include the parboiling of rice and drying, tending to children, processing of farm products such as melon, cassava, and shea butter nuts. Women are found to perform at least one or more of these activities within the courtyards daily.

It is worthy of mentioning that the courtyards of the Nupes are devoid of trees and thus the sources of shade are from those cast by the buildings. As such, activities within the courtyard are carried out systematically. The women folk during the morning hours sit on the eastern side of the courtyard under the shade provided by the rooms while the items which are being dried are placed on the western side of the compound to have the full exposure of the sun as illustrated in Figures 3.12 and 3.13.

At midday when the sun becomes very high with no much shade, the women and the children move into their rooms to take their lunch and rest. They resume back to their transactions within the courtyard when the shade begins to form on the western side due to the sun's movement towards setting in the late afternoon. The change in the location of the shade results into an exchange of space function because the women move their wares to the eastern side while they relocate to the western side of the courtyard, as illustrated in Figure 3.14.

Women under
the shade of
buildings

Farm produce
under the sun

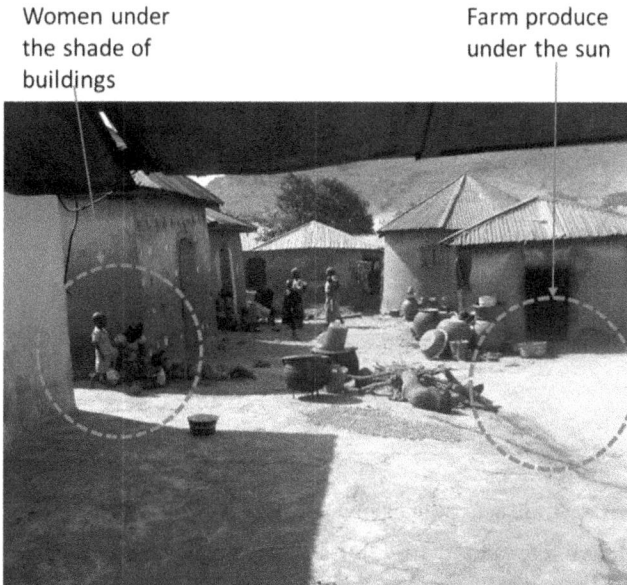

Figure 3.12: Women sitting under the shade of buildings to perform domestic chores within the courtyard.

Women sitting under
Shade provided by building

Building providing
shade

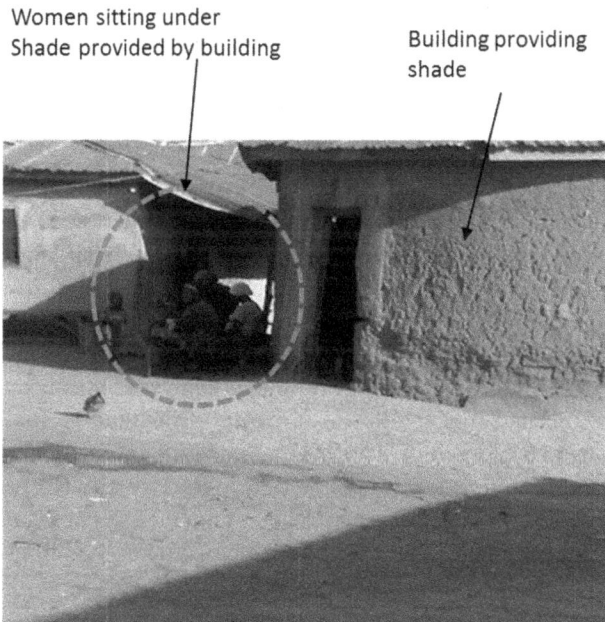

Figure 3.13: Women resting under the shade provided by the buildings and the farm products under the sun. Adopted from (Muhammad & Said 2015a).

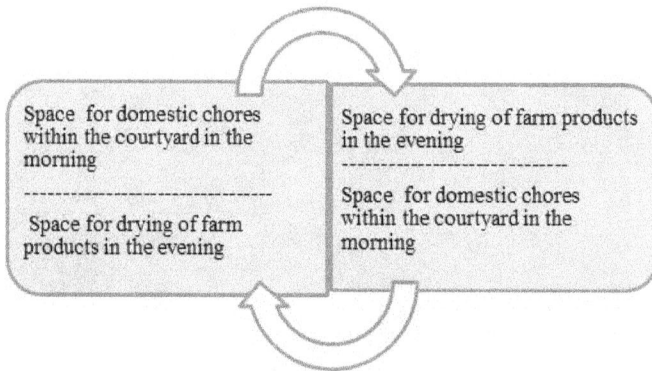

Figure 3.14: Courtyard activity diagram based on time of the day.

Although as earlier stated, the courtyards of the Nupes are devoid of trees to provide shade, this is because over time a tacit knowledge and also an adaptive behaviour in the use of the courtyard space has been developed (Muhammad and Said, 2015b) This knowledge is on how the shades are formed when the sun moves daily. Hence such tacit knowledge guides and determines the space and time for each activity within the courtyard. This implies that the Nupe people have developed a behavioural intelligence in their response to the movement of the sun and its shade formation in the courtyards.

The foregoing explained the transactions within the courtyards during the day. However, the activities of Nupe families within the courtyard continue through the night as shown in Table 3.1.

The courtyards at night serve as an extension of the rooms, especially during the hot dry period of February to May in which the temperature could be as high as 39 degrees. As such, to derive sleeping comfort, the local people have developed a climatic coping strategy through the use of courtyards as a sleeping space at night. The openness of the courtyard and the surrounding hill provides the needed cool conditions at night. During the daytime, the southwest trade wind is blocked by the topographic barrier of the hill thereby leading to warmer air on the lee wall side during the day. Landscapes with this type of scenario experience adiabatic cooler temperatures at night (Cotton *et al.*, 2011). Thus, the local people utilise such bioclimatic conditions within the courtyard for their sleeping comfort.

Table 3.1: A 24 hour, courtyard spatial transactions of families

Item	Activity(ies)	Courtyard space & locations	*Time of use	Duration
1	Breakfast, Domestic chore	Courtyard east	6 am -12 pm	6hrs
2	Drying of wares	Courtyard west	6am -12pm	6hrs
3	Resting and lunch	Bedroom	12pm -3pm	2hrs
4	Drying of wares	Courtyard east	3pm - 7pm	3hrs
5	Domestic chore,	Courtyard west	3pm - 7pm	3hrs
6	Diner	Whole courtyard	7pm – 9pm	2hr
	First phase of sleep	Whole courtyard	9pm-2am	5hrs
7	Second phase of Sleep	Bedroom	2am -5am	3hrs

*The times indicated vary between families with ± 1 hour across all activities; Adopted from (Muhammad & Said 2015a).

Sleeping within the courtyard exposes the people to mosquito inherent in the cultural landscape of Nupe community. However, this challenge of mosquito is tackled through the use of herbaceous plant called *Tammotswanagi (Ocimum gratissimum)* gotten from the immediate surrounding landscape. The fresh plant is placed in a clay pot filled with hot charcoal to produce smoke that serves as a mosquito repellent. The smoky pots are systematically placed at one end of the courtyard with wind direction studied such that the smoke blows over everyone.

Privacy is much needed, especially when sleeping at night and thus sleeping outside such an open space has the tendency of removing such privacy. Nonetheless, the absence of light at night provides the needed cover and as Appleton (1975) puts it, the interplay between light and darkness can serve as a means to the provision of refuge. As such, at night all lights are switched off and the whole courtyard becomes dark to provide privacy.

Rapoport (1969), asserts that the functionality of space utilization is based on the matrix of three variables which are an object, furniture, and man. In the cultural landscape of the Nupes, the time of the day becomes the fourth variable that determines what takes place within a given space. Time constituted in the movement of the sun, influences, where, when and what takes place in the courtyard of the Nupes. Time as a moderator of space function is also exhibited where the space used for domestic chores during the day becomes a sleeping space at night. Therefore, Nupe people have developed different strategies for the use of the courtyard during the day and night.

Furthermore, the relevance of a space can be reflected on its spatial allocation when compared to other features within the house. The survey of some compounds of the Nupe community gave a spatial output as indicated in Table 3.2

Table 3.2: The ratio of built-up spaces and courtyards.

	Compound total mean area, (n=15) m2	Compound built up area, (n=15) m2	*Courtyard space (Total area; n15)
Area	190,863	85,875	104,987
Coverage	100%	45%	55%

The spatial analysis shows that the mean total space covered by courtyard constitutes 55% of the total area of the compounds. As such the courtyard forms a high integral role in the spatial functioning of the Nupe compound (Muhammad and Said, 2015b).

Entrance hut (katamba) spatial transactions

The *katamba*, (entrance hut), serves as the main entrance into the house. Its name stems from two root words of *kata* which mean room and *mba*, the lord, thus it is literally translated as a lord's room. Generally, it is a structure that is in the custody of the *Emitso* (the compound head). *Katamba* is a symbolic entrance because most compounds of the Nupes do have several uncelebrated entrances. The *Katamba* is used by the *Emitso* to receive guests of the compound such as naming ceremonies, weddings and the mourning of the death. It is a structure of either circular or square shaped. It is simply built without windows but with two doors centrally dissecting two opposite walls, see Figure 3.15.

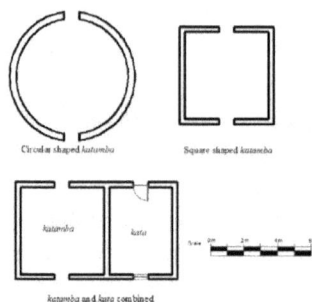

Figure 3.15: Types of katamba configurations.

The *katamba* are either built in the form of a detached structure and sometimes they are attached to other units of buildings such as bedrooms. Most *Katamba* in Nupe communities does not have windows (See Figure 3.16).

However, the entrances are left without any form of fenestration and as such this allows for cross ventilation of the space.

Figure 3.16: The square shaped katamba without a window.

Katamba is synonymous with it being used symbolically to represent compounds. This is seen in the anecdotal of a respondent, a compound head when he was giving the history of the community.

"Doko community in 1942 had 8 Katamba"

Here the number of compounds is symbolised by *katamba* and thus each compound has a *katamba* as an essential structure right from the history of the community. Further reference to *katamba* as a synonym for the compounds is also made by another respondent.

"The people of Eminndawodi are represented under the katamba of Yitsu bebi"

This means that *Eminndawodi* which is a compound on its own is merged with another compound and thus they have one representative in the village council by the person of *Yitsu bebi. Katamba* is characterised within the cultural landscape of the Nupe community to be the only structure within the compounds that maintains its original positions for a very long time. They are hardly demolished, but renovated when the need arises. This is because aside from its importance as a symbolic entrance and also a space for the receiving visitors, it also serves as a frame of reference for members of the community. Even though the frames of references are represented differently across cultures, they are required for effective communication and understanding of space-related communications (Bennardo, 2009). Similarly, for the Nupe community, it is from the *katamba* that relative references for each compound are taken. Thus, the back and side of the compounds are determined by the location of the *katamba* which is always the front irrespective of its orientation. The reference for the local compounds is thus not based on the absolute Cartesian principles of the North, South East or West.

However, despite the importance of the *katamba* in the cultural landscape of the Nupe community, a compound was found not to have one. This divergence from the general norm is attributed to two factors. Firstly, the compound was established by an Islamic immigrant who was not from Nupeland, but rather from another tribe. Secondly, the settler being an Islamic preacher built a mosque instead and therefore the mosque became the place of convergence and reference point instead of the *katamba*.

Summarily, the *katamba* in the cultural landscape of the Nupe community serves as a space and a place. Its space function lies with its use for receiving guests while its place function lies more on its symbolic representation of the compound and also a point of geographic reference.

Kata (bedroom) spatial character and transactions

The vernacular architecture of the Nupe bedrooms is such that they are mostly made up of a single small sized window of 0.6 meters by 0.6 meters, which can conventionally be construed to be inadequate to provide cross ventilation and effective lighting of the bedrooms. However, effective lighting and cross ventilation in most of the traditional rooms are attained through the combinations of the door opening and the window. The doors are always open and only fenestrated with *shegi* a traditional blind made from reed grass as illustrated in Figure 3.17.

Furthermore, it is to be noted that, the *shegi* is such not tightly weaved and as such it allows for the flow of air into and out of the bedroom.

Figure 3.17: Circular bedrooms and *shegi* blind over the door entrance; Source (Muhammad and Said, 2014).

Kata, bedrooms are spaces for rest and relaxation and therefore constitute an important space for all cultures. How these spaces are used and the form in which they are shaped is influenced by culture (De, 2016; Rapoport, 1969). Historically, in the cultural landscape of the Nupe community, *kata* has been solely shaped and constructed in circular form. However, over time the natives began to adopt the squared shapes. This is attributed to several factors amongst which are people's desire which began to change towards the need to have inner rooms and private spaces as illustrated in Figure 3.18.

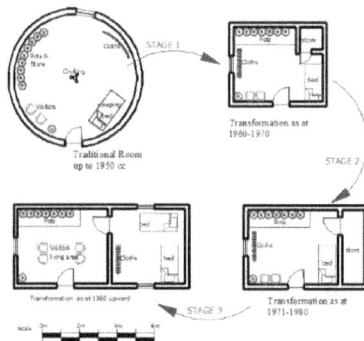

Figure 3.18: Transformation stages of bedrooms from circular to rectangular forms.

Furthermore, the influence of new roofing material from outside the community influenced the change from circular to square shaped rooms. The following is statement from a 90 years old respondent:

> *"It was difficult to have inner rooms using the circular form while at the same time the coming of zinc roofing material made it easier to roof squared shape structures".*

Deductively, the influence of new material did transform the cultural norms of the society, especially with regards to the architectural morphology. However, despite this, the influence of new methods and material did not completely change the concepts of openings. Door openings in both the circular and the squared shaped bedroom are centrally located.

The dissection of bedrooms with doors centrally is a Nupe vernacular architecture that affords the occupants some sense of privacy. This is achieved because the beds are placed at *kpakota,* the immediate space by the side of the door, mostly the right side. The door leaf is allowed to open inwards and as such, the person lying on the bed is shielded from direct visual contact of the visitor on entry into the room. Secondly, the door's central location divides the sleeping space from the visitor's space. In the like manner, a respondent also stresses the benefits of having a centrally placed door opening in the following anecdotes

> *"It is more comfortable to have the bed at the kpakota because I don't need to close the door during the day because the bed is shielded from the sun rays."*

The doors of bedrooms are always open during the day and are only covered by *shegi,* a local blind weaved from grass which allows air and light into the rooms and as such the occupants, especially during the day would prefer the most shaded spot in the bedroom which is the *kpakota.*

Comparatively, there is no distinctive size difference between the *kata* of the husband and that of the wife's. The distinction comes only in the interior furnishing of the rooms. The male bedrooms are mostly made up of the sleeping mat and a place to hang clothes while the female's bedrooms include furnishing with pots, the formation of *nanche* cooking space, a pot for drinking water and the visitor's stool. Thus, while the *kata* for the male folk is for rest that of the women functions as a place to receive visitors, a space for cooking and also place for storage of goods and valuables.

Supporting architectural features

The preceding sections discussed the values and the importance of domestic spaces in the cultural landscape of Nupe community. However, there existed some features within the domestic space that ordinarily should have constituted part of the important features of Nupe family transactions. They are the *katagi* (kitchen), edo (the granary) and the *yekun,* (local oven). Moreover, these features can be found in most of Nupe compounds. As such the questions that may be asked would be on why they seemed not to have a good measure of strengths in the daily transactions of the family members.

First, the concept of the kitchen in the cultural landscape is of two types. The first is called *nanche,* the open kitchen found within the courtyard and the *katagi,* the covered kitchen. In the cultural landscape of Nupe community, the most important economic activity of the women folk is the processing of rice, the output of the farming activities of the men folk. In the processing of rice, the women parboil and such cooking are carried out at the *nanche* (open kitchen) which is also situated within the courtyard. Secondly, the *katagi,* (covered kitchen) built for cooking of meals is mostly used when the weather is not favourable for outside cooking at the *nanche.* Such unfavourable conditions are rains and midday heavy sun. Thus, the function of the kitchen in the daily activities of the family is subsumed in the courtyard activity which is also a space where the *nanche* is situated.

Similarly, the low level of integration of the granary in the daily activity of families is attributed to several factors. Firstly, the behavioural pattern of accessing the grains from the granary is mostly carried out by the family heads on a weekly basis or fortnightly to last for the respective number of days. Secondly, grains do not constitute the only dietary plan of Nupe community. Tubers such as cassava, yam, and sweet potatoes are also important food consumed by the Nupe people which are never stored in the granary. A native farmer explains the storage principles of tubers:

> *"Cassava, sweet potatoes, and yam are harvested as the need arises because they spoil easily. We sometimes harvest all and dry them, especially when we need the plot to farm again"*

Tubers are difficult to store because they are easily affected by sprouting, rot, as well as infestation by insects and nematodes. This challenge of tuber storage is culturally attended to in two ways. One is through what can be termed as underground storage, which entails the harvest of only what is needed from the farms while the remaining are left until they are needed. However, there exist limited time for the duration of the underground storage which is limited to about three months. As such if they are not dug out, they get rotten. Therefore, the second strategy of preservation is that the locals dig the tubers out, cut them into smaller pieces and dry for use as flour for local delicacies. For example, the dried form of sweet potatoes is used as a sweetener in drinks such as *kudo,* a local non-alcoholic drink made from soaked and fermented guinea corn. Cassava on the other hand, when harvested, is processed as *nuwangi, gari,* and *rubua.* These are different intricate processes for the production of flour products from cassava for local delicacies. Therefore, while grains are stored in granaries, the process of preservation of tubers is through adaptive preservation of underground storage at the farm and also through the local production process of drying. This shows that the culinary traditions of the Nupe people have an effect on the spatial transactions with built forms.

Again, one of the supporting architectural features which are found within the domestic space in all Nupe compounds is the *yekun* (see Figure 3.19 and 3.20).

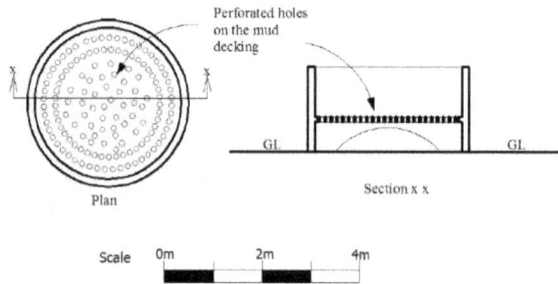

Figure 3.19: The plan and cross section of yekun (traditional Oven).

Figure 3.20: The elevation and interior view of the *yekun,* traditional hearth.

The *yekun* is cylindrically shaped and built with clay. It measures about 1.6 meters in height and a meter in diameter. Even though *yekun* is found in almost all Nupe compounds, its non-integration in the daily activities of the families is associated with its seasonal use. To illustrate, the first crop to be reaped is the bulrush millet, which is harvested in the middle of the raining season. Drying them for immediate consumption under the sun is very difficult. *Yekun*, therefore, is used to quickly dry the much awaited first crop of the season, the bulrush millet *for* immediate consumption. Another seasonal use of *yekun* is the shea nut roasting, which is also within the raining season. Roasting of shea nuts constitutes part of the process for the production of *mikote*. *Mikote* is an oil which is used locally for cooking and also exported for industrial uses in the production of cosmetics. Thus, for the womenfolk of most families, the *yekun* forms an important feature within the domestic space, but it is only required at specific periods of the year. One striking observation is that despite the limited period of use annually, each family head ensures that there is at least one *yekun* that is kept in good shape. A family head's statement in the anecdote below further showcases the value of *yekun* in the cultural landscape:

> *"My father built the yekun outside the compound, he has to ensure that it is in good shape, we will not like to go to another compound to use their own"*

There exists some sense of pride to own *yekun* in each compound, even though it is a shared facility within a compound, the local people hardly cross over to another compound to use. It is considered as ineptitude by the male folk not to have at least one *yekun*. The *yekun* therefore, despite its limited utilization, it constitutes a sense of pride to the Nupe people to have one in each compound.

Summary

Summarily, the transactions of the Nupe family within the domestic space are conceptualized differently between male and females as well as the children. Each of these people has preferences towards the use of spaces. Furthermore, vernacular architecture is constituted both in tangible and intangible form. The intangible spaces are such that they do not constitute major transactions of the local people; however, the presence of such features portrays a sense of pride. Also, to be noted is that the utilization of spaces and their functions are time-dependent.

Chapter 4

Transactions of Indigenous Professions

Farming in Nupe community

Rural communities in Africa depend mostly on subsistence agricultural practices for sustenance (Dzanku, 2015). This is not different in Doko community. As a matter of fact, the importance and also dependence on farming are found to be exhibited in all of the community's transactions. It is a common phenomenon to hear the locals discuss about their farms such as the expected time of harvest and the expected yield from the farm inputs. Similarly, prayers are also held for good yields and for a stable rainfall. As such people's transactions are also found extending to natural forces such as rain because the sustenance of the community depends on it.

Most Nupe communities practice the hoe agriculture system and thus the use of heavy equipment such as tractor is not common. Hoe agriculture requires a lot of effort for a considerable piece of plot to be cultivated. While the more industrialised communities use mechanically driven equipment on their farms, the less developed communities use animal power, such as camel, cows, and donkey to drive their tools on the farms. Contrastingly, the Nupe community has culturally developed a driving force for their farming activities called *dzoro.*

Dzoro is a system of co-operative farm work that is made up of a number of people ranging from 5 to 20 persons. In this system of co-operative farming, works are carried out on individual farm plots of those that make up the team on a rotational basis. This makes it possible for a large expanse of land to get worked on at once. However, the people that constitute the team do not necessarily have the same size of plots nor do their farms have the same ease or difficulty of cultivation. Despite this, the Nupe farmers have a system that takes care of this, as explained by a native farmer respondent in this anecdote:

> *"We are twelve in my Dzoro, but when it was my turn to weed my farm, I asked for only 7 persons"*

Here the farmer knows that a seven-manpower is enough to weed his farm and thus he called for only seven people. The remaining five people are reserved for other farm activities such as harvesting at the same farm or work at another farm. The farmers sometimes even transfer such labour to another farming season. Equally important are the monetization values associated with *dzoro* labour. It is such that a person can sell off his labour force to a willing buyer. Here the labour force goes to work for another person and the money is given to the person that sold the *dzoro*. This situation is common and the reason that can give rise to this is exemplified by a 40-year-old farmer:

"I needed money to buy fertilizer for my farm and it was getting late, so I had to sell my dzoro to Madu"

Similarly, *dzoro* is transferable and can be offered as a gift, as explained by another respondent, age 27:

"My father in-law's farm needed to be weeded and therefore I took my dzoro to the farm"

Here the young farmer saw an opportunity to present a gift to his father-in-law through *dzoro*. *Dzoro* in a Nupe community is constituted in three forms. They are *sakafugi, lati-yan-efo, and lozungi*, which means the break of dawn, morning and evening respectively. These are periods marked by the people to work on their farms within the day as illustrated in Table 4.1.

Table 4.1: The schedule of *dzoro*, the daily Farming Periods

Name	Meaning	Period	Duration
Sakafugi	Morning	6am-8am	2 hours
Lati-yan-efo	Afternoon	9am- 4pm	6 hours
Lozungi	Evening	5pm-7pm	2 hours

Dzoro in Nupe community is constituted by any or combination of the schedules illustrated in Table 4.1. It is such that a person could belong to *Lati-yan-efo* in one group and *lozungi* in another group. Such is the matrix of *dzoro* concepts of farming in Nupe communities. This traditional cultural ability of the Nupe people is as a result of accumulated knowledge of the co- evolution of nature and culture (Adams, 2010). This is because it is within the human ability to understand the natural environment for his sustenance. Part of such knowledge is the understanding of the landscape for an effective agricultural practice of farming. Such knowledge of the landscape over a period of time results in the development of a native calendar as portrayed in Table 4.2.

Table 4.2: Doko Nupe community farming calendar and landscape indicators

Native calendar	Farm operation	Landscape indicator
Month One (March)	Preparation of yam plots -Sowing of bulrush	Appearance of gbama (reddish insect)
Month Two (April)	-Sowing of millet -Sowing of groundnut -Harvesting of bulrush millet	-Locust bean trees start to fruit -Mango trees begin to fruit -Appearance of (kparogi bird) (Partridge bird -Caging of goats and sheep
Month Three (May)	-Planting of sweet potatoes -Planting of melon -Planting of upland cassava	-Appearance of *mani-mani* greenish -yellowish maggot
Month Four (June)	Harvesting of the first yam	-Shea trees begin to fruits
Month Five (July)	-Planting of beans begins on the high land -Preparing the flood plain fields and planting of rice begins	Some flood plains get flooded
Month Six (August)	-All flood plains are planted with rice -Sweet potatoes harvest - melon harvested	Most flood plains get flooded, providing opportunity for washing of melon
Month Seven (September)	Harvest of corn	The immediate landscape surrounding the compounds begins to look bare devoid of vegetation.
Month Eight (October)	-Second yam harvest -Harvesting of inland cassava	Some floodplain begins to dry, Appearance of monkeys
Month Nine (November)	-Harvest of rice begins -Harvesting of groundnut -Harvest of guinea corn	Disappearance of monkeys
10th Month (December)	-Harvest of rice completed Harvest of beans on the inland	Appearance of cattle herds and Cattle Egret (Bubulcus ibis) white bird
Month 11 (January)	Burning of farms	The landscape becomes dry and dusty Goats and sheep release on free range
Month 12 (February)	Burning and clearing of land go on	The landscape becomes dry and dusty

The first month of the native calendar occurs around March every year. This month marks the beginning of the cropping season. At this period, the fields get cleared and the yam ridges and bulrush millet are planted. Part of the landscape indicator for the period is the appearance of a reddish insect called *gbama* within is found within the community's landscape. The second month comes with landscape indicators such as the fruiting of the locust bean trees, caging of free-ranging domestic animals such as goats and sheep. The bulrush millet, which takes 40 days to get ripe, begins to mature and this attracts the appearance of partridge bird which feeds on it. The challenge of these birds thus makes it inherent for the crops to be planted within a short walking distance from the houses. The close proximity of planting the bulrush millet is such that young boys and girls can be sent to the fields to scare off the birds. The children do this through the use of available material found within the landscape such as empty cans. The empty cans are struck with sticks to make the desired noise and sound. As a result of this, the landscape becomes filled with the sounds of drums and songs of the children as they contribute their quota in their respect family farming activity for 7 to 9 days. What is to be noted is that the type of crop determines the distance away from home where it is planted. More also is that, since children are the ones engaged in the process of the physical control of bulrush millet from the pests (birds), the crops are therefore planted near the immediate vicinity of the community to allow ease of commuting to and from the homes of the young ones.

Similarly, as part of the strategy for the control of the bird pest, the community as a whole ensures that their bulrush millets are planted at the same time and harvested at the same time. This is because the bulrush millet is the first crop of the seasons and therefore it is a very important crop to the local people as indicated by a respondent in this quotation:

> *"Kpayi, the bulrush millet is fast to mature, easy to cultivate and also it could be used to prepare different kinds of food while we await other crops to mature."*

In the cultural landscape, *kpayi* is a crop that is drought resistant and thus has a minimal risk of failure as such in situations where other crops such as maize and guinea corn fail, the locals fall back to the bulrush millet. The bulrush in its fresh form could be roasted and taken directly; it could be grounded into flour for the preparation of porridge, and other forms of local dishes. Immediately after the harvest of the bulrush, the farmers begin to plant sweet potatoes, cassava and melon which are mostly planted for domestic consumption except for the melon which is planted in large scale for sales in the market. It is also within this period that the landscape becomes filled with the appearance of *mani-mani* (greenish yellowish maggot) which feeds on the leaves of the *Butryspernum parkii* (Shea nut tree). In this case, the women folks go to the fields to pick the *mani-mani* which is processed and used in the preparation of local dishes. The process involves boiling and then either fried immediately or allowed to dry under the sun and some days later, it could be used to prepare vegetable soups or eaten directly. The fifth month is for the harvest of yam and this period is associated with the fruiting of the Shea butter tree. Here again, the women go to the field to pick the shea nuts, which are taken back home to be dried and used for the production of oils called *mikote*. The sixth month is when beans and melon are harvested respectively. This is followed by the flooding of the flood plains which provides an opportunity for the women folk to wash melon seeds see Figure 4.1.

Figure 4.1: Women washing melon seed in the floods

Concurrently, the fifth, sixth and seventh local months; (July, August, and September) are associated with the cultivation of rice on the flood plains. The cultivation of rice fields depends on the floods from river Niger which overflows its banks seasonally. The flow of the flood requires that the farmer makes ridges with consideration given to the direction of the flood. Small ridges *gbara* of about 15-20cm thick are made parallel to the direction of the flood while bigger ridges called *gbagbako* of about 30-60cm thick are made across as embankments. This is to allow for the smaller ridges to get flooded (Figures 4.2, 4.3 and 4.4). The control of the flood is made through the small openings (floodgates) on the main ridges as the farmers deem them fit from time to time.

Figure 4.2: A freshly ploughed ridges awaiting the flood

Figure 4.3: The farm ridges gradually getting flooded

Figure 4.4: A fully flooded rice farm

The importance of having the small ridges flooded has an advantage as stated in this anecdote:

"When you control and ensure that the gbara is always flooded, it prevents weeds from growing"

The weeding of rice fields constitutes a difficult task and as such the farmers would prefer to monitor and control the level of water to ensure that the field is completely flooded to prevent weeds from growing. This is achieved through the use of the floodgates. While this continues, the rice matures and gets harvested in the eighth and ninth month. Similarly, at the ninth month, the corn gets harvested on the uplands. The landscape begins to see the appearance of monkeys, which pest on the matured cassava, groundnut, and guinea corn while the farmers harvest these crops. After harvest, the landscape becomes dry on the tenth month while the egret bird which accompanies the cattle takes over the landscape to feed on the roughages left on the farms. Similarly, domestic animals such as the goats and sheep are released in the eleventh and twelfth month before the next season's first rain when they become domesticated.

The continuous engagement with the landscape in farming activities over a long period of time has made the local people develop the concept of time to suit their farming activities. This is portrayed in the floodplain which does not strictly depend on the rainfall, but rather on when the plots get flooded. In the flood plains, the farmers read the time for cultivation directly from the landscape. The farming system of the Nupe community is generally associated with a series of interwoven activities between the upland and floodplain farming activities. The farms in the flood plains depend on the level of floods for cultivation, while those on the uplands depend directly on rainfall and also inclined to the series of activities which begins with the planting of bulrush and ends with the harvest of beans and late maturing guinea corn.

Accordingly, farm labour within the cultural landscape is developed to cope with the cultivation of a large expanse of land through *dzoro* the cooperative farming. Different adaptive strategies are developed by the local people to cope with the natural phenomena such as the flood, through their cultural farming strategy of *gbara* and *gbagbako* formation. Certain crops are planted based on distance and location to suit the participatory role of the children in the farming activity. Consequently, the farming activities of the community are culturally influenced and adapted to suit local people's needs.

Traders and landscape transactions

Trade serves as a means for the exchange of goods and services within communities. These normally take place in the market. In the cultural landscape of Doko community, women dominate the greater percentage of the market scene. Even though the farm produce is mainly the product of the men, the women are the ones that take them to the market for sales. This is the social division of labour between the men and the women in the cultural landscape of the Nupe community. This also transcends down to the female children who are also seen to mimic the market scene as they play at home. Thus, the market environment forms part of the process of nurturing of the young ones. Children are therefore culturally shaped by what they see their older generation do. In fact, the art of trading by the girls is a valuable skill that needs to be acquired as she is expected to become a good marketer of her husband's farm products when she gets married. The operation of the economy is such that the women are more involved with the liquid cash than the men. The agricultural product, which is rice after each harvest season serves as the working capital for the women. Some percentage of the total harvest is given to the wife and from it; she is expected to manage it for the basic needs of the family such as groceries, and cosmetics. A family head asserts as follows:

> *"Last year's harvest was good, so I gave my wife eight bags of rice. I have to borrow out of it to repair my motorcycle this year"*

This anecdote depicts the system of family upkeep within the cultural landscape. The women are the managers of the resources of the family that stems from the men's farm works. Thus, the economics of the village are culturally constituted to have women as the traders and the men as the producers. This is in contrast to what is found in the culture of the Hausa community of Northern Nigeria (Muhammad-Oumar, 1997; Nwanodi, 1989). For the Hausa culture, the economic activities of the womenfolk are within the boundary of their homes while the men do the market transactions. This thus depicts the cultural distinction of each cultural landscape in terms of role plays in economic transactions.

Gozan – (barber-doctor) transactions

Gozan, to the Nupes, means a barber and the doctor combined into one profession. They are involved with the performance of surgeries in the form of circumcisions, shaving of the head, administration of oral medication and as well as the spiritual treatment of ailments. The performance of both head shaving and surgical works is carried out using *efin*, a blade locally made from aluminium.

The *efin* is the primary tool of the *Gozan*, and it forms the window of initiation into the profession of *Gozan*. This is expressed by the *Ndasonkyara* (, the head of *gozan* in his narrations as follows:

> *"The first thing that my grandfather who was then Ndasonkyara, asked me to do was to sharpen the blunt blade. I kept on sharpening the blunt blade for several days until it became sharp enough to cut the skin."*

Sharpening of *efin* forms the first act of introduction into *gozan*. It is expected that familiarity and the skills of handling the blade is an important aspect of the journey into becoming a *gozan*. Apprenticeship forms part of the process of acquisition of the skills to become a *gozan*. A young person is attached with the master *gozan* in which he learns through observation while he gets to practice intermittently on a child's head.

After the perfection in the shaving of the head, the apprentice *gozan* is then taught the act of cutting tribal marks and then circumcision. These acts of shaving and, cutting of tribal marks constitute the primary skills that certify a person to be called gozan as asserted by the *Ndasonkyara* in the anecdote below:

> *"The day I was asked to circumcise a boy, whom I successful carried out gave me some joy because I knew from that day that I had become a gozan."*

Furthermore, the apprentice during the process of learning to become a
gozan, he is taught the preparation of herbal medicines which also form part
of the concoctions applied on the wounds and circumcision.

As earlier stated, one of the functions of the gozan in Nupe community is
the performance of circumcisions. It is carried out within the Nupe community in groups, such that children within the age group of 3 to 6 years are gathered together within the community and circumcised. Children are never told
the day on which such circumcisions are to be carried out in order to prevent
them from evading. The day for such activity is mostly known by the compound head and the gozan who will carry out the surgery on male children.
Children are picked up early before the breaks of dawn from their beds are
lured into a room one by one. Thereafter, the children are then picked one
after the other for the circumcision. The circumcision involves the removal of
the foreskin of the male genitals with *efin* which takes about 6 minutes. After
the removal of the foreskin, *gabaruwan kasa*, a locally prepared herb, is applied to the wound as narrated by the *Ndasonkyara*

> "The herb we apply to circumcised children's genitals is gabaruwan
> kasa, with the mixture of ningoro powder, and bafin"

The local herb major ingredient is *gabarunwan kasa* (*Charmaecrista mimo-
soides*) other ingredients include *ningoro*, (the locust bean powder, pulp), and
bafin, the *Piliostigma thonningii*. The mixture when applied to a wound is
said to heal it within 8 days. Modern hospitals encourage circumcision of
children some few weeks after birth. Contrastingly, within the culture of the
Nupe community, it is preferred to have such circumcision carried out when
the child is older from the age of 3 to 5 years. The cultural values derivable
from such delay of circumcision are explained by a compound head in this
anecdote:

> "The circumcision of boys when they are a little bit older allows them to
> value pain"

Circumcision of children at infancy may not necessarily be said to be pain-
less, but at that age, they are not much aware of what is happening. The value
of pain within the context of circumcision of the Nupe people means that the
children will know that it is painful to let blood out of the human body. As
such it is believed that children will ensure they are careful not to indulge in
activities that will cause physical injuries either on themselves or other people. The question that arises is how the girls within the community get to
learn the value of pain, this a family head explains as follows:

"The girls are naturally more docile than the boys and also they are not as adventurous as the boys"

Deductively, the boys within the cultural landscape are understood to be more adventurous and therefore are exposed to more risk of injuries than the girls. Therefore, it is better to have them circumcised when they are much older. If the essence of late circumcision is to allow the boys to appreciate pain, then it can be argued that there exist an imbalance between the boys and the girls within the community. This is because; there exist some cultures that do female circumcision, which is linked to female purity and cleanliness (Biglu *et al.*, 2016). Even though these female circumcisions are based on different cultural value, the Nupe community does not have female circumcision and as such the girls do not experience the value of pain.

However, for male folks, there exists another social value derived from the age group circumcision. It is a social value which allows for an age group classification, this is deduced from a respondent in this quotation:

"Ndagi and Sani are age mates because they were circumcised together"

Nupe community is constituted such that keeping track of people's age forms part of the cultural norm. Leadership is made or given based on age, while at the same time respect is also accorded based on age. For example, it is expected that young person greets the older person first and also when an errand is to be taken within a group of people, the youngest goes for the errand. The norm in which respects are accorded to elders ensures that age group monitoring is made through various means which also include the time of circumcision.

The leadership of the local barbers who is called *Ndasonkyara* extends beyond the immediate community of Doko. The family of *Konufu* is the sole custodian of the gozan practice. Hence the family continues to pass the skills from one generation to another. Thus, within the immediate cultural landscape and the surrounding villages, the *konufu* family is always called upon to render their services. *Ndasonkyara*, the head of the *gozan* guild affirms this as follows:

"Well, I can tell you that all the members of this community were circumcised in this our compound"

Conversely, this assertion of all the members of the community being circumcised by the family of *konufu* people only holds true up to the early 1980's. This is because government clinics were established and people began to shift to the use of these clinics for the circumcision of their male children. This, however, does not completely rule out the local circumcision method because some members still prefer the traditional method. The leadership guild is such that the *Ndasonkyara* controls 24 communities from far and near, they are Doko, Efako, Boku, Emigba, Kopa, Dingi, Mambe Tako, Mambe Tiffin, Fokpo Batagi, Gbade, Dzowu, Dofu, Sossa, Sa'ati, Nuwon Dzurugi, Guduko, Ndashaba, Goga, Nuwon Dzurigi, Vunchi, and Egubagi. For this reason, the *gozan* were found to leave their home for several days and weeks as they travel from one village to another to offer their services. The *Ndasonkyara* further explains:

> *"There was a time when in this our compound the gozan were no more than three and as such when they leave for such works they spend weeks out of the house as they move from one village to another"*

All these communities mentioned are located within the radius of 25 kilometres. However, because the movement was historically done on foot, it took very long hours of walk to get to some communities. It thus necessitated the *gozan,* staying in each village visited until they finish attending to the community's needs for that period. Over time, the long absence from home began to reduce because *Konufu* family began to train more of its family members. Furthermore, also is the means of travelling which got improved through the use of bicycles and motorcycles. The *Ndasonkyara* explains further:

> *"We are plenty and as such, all the communities mentioned earlier are distributed amongst us and each person is allocated a village.*

This thus forms the leadership structure of the *Gozan,* and even though it is a skill highly demanded within the community, the skill is maintained and held on strongly only within a single family. This is different from what is obtainable even within the neighbouring community of Bida where such skills of *Gozan* could be learnt by an outsider (Nadel, 1942).

Medicinal rituals of the community-*wasa*

Ritual is an established procedure in the performance of traditional cultural observance (Mbito and Malia, 2009). The rituals found in Doko community are two types, the fixed and contingent rituals. The contingent rituals are those performed in the form of emergency. An example of a contingent ritual is performed to cure a person supposedly stroke by *radi*. *Radi* is believed as an ailment caused by evil forces of thunder strike. Contingent rituals are privately performed while the fixed rituals are open to the public such as the *wasa* performance. *Wasa* in the words of *Ndasonkyara* is performed on the second

Sunday of the eight months of Nupe calendar. It comes with ceremonies and a process that has to be meticulously followed by members that partake in it.

Wasa ritual involves the use of several condiments of tree leaves, barks, root and also some parts of the animals such as the snake's head. Amongst the function of *wasa* are its use as an antidote against snake bites, a cure for stomach ache, and it is also used for protection against theft. Meanwhile, for the Nupes, *wasa* is a ritual process for the preparation of medicine and also the name of the medicine itself. The preparation of *wasa* is performed by only the Konufu household. As such the knowledge is kept within the enclave of the household and transferred from one generation to another. The process starts with the assembly of male members of the family on the scheduled fixed date early in the morning at the hut of the *Ndasonkyara*. It is from his hut that the team set out to the forest for the collection of the condiments for the preparation of *wasa*. The process is a meticulous one as *Ndasonkyara* (R5) explains in the following anecdote:

> "The digging of the roots is not done ordinarily; certain roots are dug with hands carefully such that the roots are dug up to the tip without allowing it to break. After the main root is dug with the hands, all other ones are then dug using hoes or other implements available"

The procedure is such that a particular type of tree root is dug out with bare hands. It is ensured that the first part of the root to be dug does not break right down to the tip. This the *Ndasonkyara*, the head of the team does by himself and after a successful digging of the first root, he then gives instruction for the digging of other species of roots using implements such as hoes and cutlasses. After the required quantities of the roots are collected, the team sets back to home with the roots for the next stage of the ritual. However, during the journey back home some strict code of conduct is observed by the team. It is forbidden for the members in the procession to talk to any person on their way back home except within themselves. On reaching home, the roots are all heaped together at the courtyard close to the *Ndasonkyara* hut.

At home, the roots are cut into smaller pieces by the young male members of the family and set ready to be fired up in the evening. At 7 pm the whole household assembles for the final stage of the *wasa* preparation. The female members of the family also contribute their own quota to the collection of firewood on an earlier day from the farms. The firewood is made up of the combination of dry and wet wood. Two large earthen pots enough to take 50 litres of water are placed in the bunker with the collections of the roots inside the pots and set ablaze. The mixture of dry wood with the fresh ones in the setting up of the fire bunker is done on purpose. This is explained by respondent in this quotation:

"The firewood is made up of the combination of fresh and dry wood such that the fire does not burn too fast."

The process requires that the roots are charred inside the pot gradually for some time. The process of charring starts around 7 pm and continued into the early hours of the following morning before the break of dawn at 4 am. As such, it is a slow and long night for the preparation of *wasa*. However, the long night is filled up with entertainment by the community drummers who continued to sing and beat their drums from beginning to the end of the ritual. What is to be noted is that *wasa* ritual is performed in the open and thus the members of the community are free to observe and also get entertained. Markedly, *Wasa* ritual is categorised into three distinctive levels of participation. The first stage is exclusively for the initiated which is only made up of elders of the *konufu* which includes some sacred ritual performed before setting out to go to the forest for the collections of the condiments as well as the first herb/root to be collected by the *Ndasonkyara* himself. The second stage involves the participation of some members of the konufu family in digging other species of roots after the first has been dug. The third stage is the entertainment aspect which allows members of the community to join in its performance. By and large, the whole *wasa* ritual ends when the content inside the pots placed on the fire bunker becomes completely charred. Thereafter, the charred content is poured out into large bales and given to the women in the family to pound into powder. The powdery substance is then taken to the *Ndasonkyara* for safe keep and use when the need arises.

It is worth mentioning that the performance of *wasa* ritual takes place on a specific spot. This is attributed to the observance of a strict code of practice which ensures that the site and place, fulfil certain conditions for the *wasa* process to take place. Once a place is chosen, it seldom changes, *Ndasonkyara* explains in this quotation;

"We don't change the spot for the preparation of wasa anyhow, however, when the need arises, we shift, but we have to perform some rituals seeking for the permission for the change."

It is a cultural belief that *wasa* knows when its place of performance needs to be shifted out of necessity and thus would not mind. A close look at the space for the performance of the *wasa* ritual does not show any mark or indication of sacredness. This is because after the performance the whole place becomes devoid of any object and thus normal activities such as children play, and adults resting under the shade of the tree near the spot continue to take place over the same space. Deductively, *Wasa* ritual constitutes a tangible ritual performance and provides medicine for the community of Doko as a whole. There exists no any physical structure built for its performance. However, it is associated with the creation of an intangible space and place for its performance within the cultural landscape of the Nupe community. Cultural rituals constituted in the form of festivals most times do provide an emblematic cultural heritage *(del Barrio, et al., 2012)*. This emblematic heritage is also exemplified in the *wasa* rituals of the Nupe community in tangible and intangible forms. The intangible value is experienced at a particular time and expires at the moment the final product is made. While tangible value is drawn from the medicinal product which is used for the treatment of ailments in the community.

Natural landscape transactions

The natural landscape has an influence in the formation of settlements such that its character constitutes one of the key factors considered by people before settlements are established. Appleton (1975) asserts that the main criteria for the establishment of settlement revolve round prospect and refuge. Similarly, the output of empirical evidence of the studied community showcases the hill, natural water bodies, and trees as the most valuable features in which the prospects and refuge of the Nupe cultural transactions are constituted. How these three features constitute cultural values of the Nupe community are discussed in the following sections.

Cultural values of the hill

A first-time visitor to the community (Doko) would always be attracted to the giant hill which seems to swallow and places the entire village, in a valley. The hill runs from the southeastern region down to the north -western region of the community (See Figure 4.5 and 4.6).

The history of the community is tied the hill. The community is said to be a conglomeration of different clans who sought refuge from the persistent wars and slavery that was common in the region during the early 18th century wars (Idrees, 1998). The communities which were from the *Edoko* and *Dazhi* clan left their settlements far away from the hill and decided to settle at the base of the hill which offered a vantage position of security. This is further buttressed by a community elder, aged 75 in the following quotation:

> *"The Fulani war was a common phenomenon and the neighbouring villages were constantly raided, our fathers decided to move up close to the hill together with the Dazhi clan"*

Figure 4.5: The south-eastern end of Doko hill

Figure 4.6: The view of the hill from the centre of the community

The mention of the Fulani here could be due to the Islamic propagation headed by the Fulani jurists who were actively involved in the propagation of Islamic religion from the far northern Nigeria down to the middle belts in the early 18th century (Musa, 2004). Thus, these invasions as feared by the community can be attributed not only to the wars but also to the acculturation of Islamic culture in the community. This can be attributed to the fact that the Nupe community already had an established traditional religion of *gunu* (Nadel, 1954). As such the coming of another religion would have posed as a threat. Furthermore, there existed more conditions provided by the landscape around the hill that attracted settlement. The hillside was fertile for agriculture and so also was the presence of water. Furthermore, the vantage point of the hill provided refuge, as such all the basic components for the establishment of a settlement was present. This is further buttressed by respondent, age 80 years:

"Even though the hill was rocky, it was very fertile and thus a small portion cultivated provided a good yield".

The system of agriculture practice, on the hill, involved the use of terrace farming strategy. The strategy involves the creation of ridges which are made parallel to the slope so as to reduce the effect of washing off of ridges and the nutrients down to the valley. The rocky and sloppy nature of the hill as shown in Figure 4.7 would have been termed unsuitable, however, security was paramount, and thus the community instead developed a farming method to cultivate their crops. The hill, therefore, provided the refuge for security and prospect for food.

Similarly, water is essential for the establishment of communities. It is needed first for the biological needs and then for other domestic chores. For the community, the source of water was attributed to the natural pools that existed at the base of the hill as explained by a respondent aged 80 below:

"When our grandfathers came there were three major water sources, one was called beria, the next one gbenia and the third was gadunchita. They were all natural pools and therefore wells were never dug, and that was what made our grandfather settle at the hillside"

The availability of water contributed to the stay at the hill more also that it was a natural spring. This is because digging of wells would have been very cumbersome, especially with the limited technology available as well as the rocky nature of the hill. Summarily, the establishment of Doko community showcased that security, water and source of food were the primary determinants as illustrated in Figure 4.8.

Figure 4.7: The steep and rocky nature of Doko hill

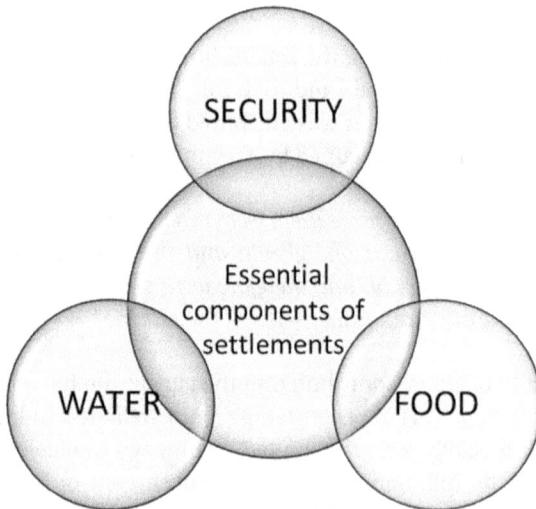

Figure 4.8: The primary determinants for the establishment of settlements

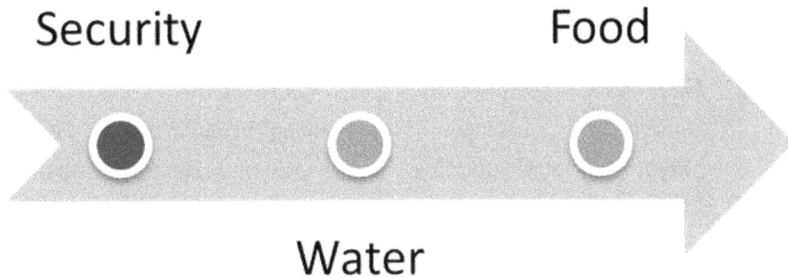

Figure 4.9: The hierarchy of needs in the establishment of settlements

Equally important as illustrated in Figure 4.9 is that within the three attributes for the establishment of settlements, security of lives and properties comes first, followed by the presence of water in the landscape and then food.

Cultural landscape values of trees

Trees are one of the most important vegetative elements of a landscape. They play important roles in the lives of those who inhabit the landscape. The values associated with the trees could be both tangible and intangible thus, values of trees depend on the culture of the people. As such, for a cultural landscape, values are best measured through the perceptions of the people who inhabit the landscape. And in doing so the following sections will discuss how trees are valued in both tangible and intangible forms within the cultural landscape of the Nupe community. Firstly, the physical spatial distribution and types of tree species found planted is discussed, followed by the cultural values associated with them.

Spatial distribution of trees

The survey of all the compounds visited (n=54) shows that 88 percent of Doko compound have trees. And out of this total number of compounds, the location in which the trees were planted is mostly in front near the katamba at 75%. This was followed by the back at 18% and the remaining 7% found distributed in some courtyards.

Furthermore, the species of trees found within the community's compounds are summarily presented in Table 4.3.

Table 4.3: Species of Trees Found in the Compounds

Sn	Local name	Common name	Scientific name	Percentage
1	*Lemu*	Orange	*Citrus sinensis*	39%
2	*Gbanchi*	Ficus	*Ficus platyphylla*	12%
3	*Mungoro*	Mango	*Mangifera indica*	11%
4	*Kochi*	Shea Butter Tree	*Butyrospermum parkii*	9%
5	*Goyiba*	Guava	*Psidium guava*	8%
6	*Nimu*	Neem Tree	*Azadirachta indica*	8%
7	*Yikunu*	Coconut Tree	*Elaeis guineensis*	5%
8	*Yaba*	Banana	*Musa specie*	5%
9	*Konkeni*	Pawpaw	*Carica papaya*	3%

Adopted from Muhammad & Said 2014, page 275

Table 4.3 showcases seven out of nine species of trees within the Nupe community landscape are fruit trees Lemu (*Citrus sinensis).* Orange is the most common tree because it provided fruits as well as shade for relaxation all year round. The only non-fruit trees planted were *gbanchi (Ficus platyphylla)* and *nimu (Azadirachta indica).* The choice of *gbanchi* is due to its fast growth while *nimu* provides shade all year round. Furthermore, the preference of Orange over other fruit trees is explained by a respondent (R10) in this anecdote:

> *"We need the shade from the orange tree because it grows fast and also produces fruits, so we planted it"*

Fast growth and the production of fruit formed an important reason for the choice of trees to be planted. The orange, mango and Ficus trees are the most predominant trees found in front of the compounds. They are respectively called *lemu, mungoro* and *gbanchi.* The foregoing showcases the spatial distribution of trees within the community landscape. More also is that spatial transactions are also part of the values derivable from the trees. In Nupe narratives, the addition of *"ta"* at the end of any plant differentiates and also qualifies such plant to mean a place. So, in this case, *lemu* becomes *lemuta*, *mungoro* becomes *mungorota* and *gbanji* become *gbanchita.* Such are the qualifications given to trees when they become a space and a place. For example, a statement made as follows;

"Madu shi mungorota"

It means that Madu is under the mango tree, however, its meaning is not only literal, but it indicates that the tree has become a space of social transaction, (see Figure 4.10).

Figure 4.10: People sitting under the shade of a mango for social transaction

Trees in Nupe communities constitutes a place where people congregate for meetings, play for the children and sometimes simple commercial transactions. Similarly, memories of social transactions are tied to trees and the shades they provide. For example, during the course of discussion with a respondent, he associated his childhood to the play under the tree and in doing so he mentioned some of the friends he played with.

"We played together under the gbanchita with Bakar, Ndagi, and Musa, we were very close"

As such, play under the tree constitutes part of the everyday space for children within Nupe community cultural landscape. In doing so memories are kept and recalled similarly, they are able to classify their age groups in terms of mates, juniors and seniors. The foregoing are values associated with the physical trees found within the immediate landscape of the compounds. The next section discusses the transactions of the Nupe people with tree species that are not necessarily found in the compounds, but at the farms. As such the cultural values of trees are constituted mostly in an intangible form.

Intangible values of trees

The values of trees are not necessarily limited to their physical presence within the everyday landscape of communities. As such the most appropriate means towards the understanding of such intangible values of trees requires direct enquiry from the natives. Consequent upon this, the output of the questions on respondents between ages of 25 to 85 on the values of trees within the cultural landscape of Nupe community is shown in Table 4.4.

A total number of 22 tree species were mentioned. *Wuchi (Khaya senegalensis)*, recorded the highest count followed by *Kulanchi (Crateva adansonii)* both indigenous with a count of 42 and 24, respectively. *Wuchi* is traditionally valued for its medicinal properties, the bark, which is made into decoction is for the treatment of fever, skin diseases, body pain, blood stimulation and also in the treatment of menstrual cramps.

The root of *kulanchi* is culturally believed to cure skin cancer. The roots are dried, milled and taken with porridge and also applied to the affected area of the skin. The next set of trees with high count values is *goyiba (Psidium guajava)*, *nimu (Azadirachta indica)*, *kpache (Terminalia schimperina)* and *kokeni (Carica papaya)*. The decoction of leaves from any three of the four aforementioned tree species is also used culturally to cure malaria. Deductively, trees with the highest cultural values are those associated with the treatment of malaria. This is because; malaria is endemic in paddy growing communities (Namsa *et al.*, 2011). As such all trees associated with the treatment of malaria within the context of the cultural landscape are highly valued. Furthermore, tree species with economic values within the Nupe community are *lonchi (Parkia biglobosa)*, and *eko (Butryspernum parkii)*. *Lonchi* is a native tree that grows up to 12 meters high. It is deciduous with a very thick bark and produces fruit in the form of pods which contains a yellowish flour pulp. The seeds are used locally in the preparation of *kula*, a traditional soup seasoning condiments, while the yellowish powder from the fruit is used for the preparation of porridge called *elonuwa*. *Elonuwa* is prepared by the mix of guinea corn flour with the hot extract of the yellowish powder. *Butryspernum parkii* is also traditionally popular for its edible soft skin while the nuts are used in the preparation of shea nut oil. The fruits are allowed to fall naturally and they are picked by women in their respective family farms. The nuts are dried and the shells removed through shelling to expose the soft seeds. It is from the pounding and grinding of the seeds that shea oil is produced which is both used for cooking and cosmetics. However, most families do not go into the stage of oil production, rather the seeds are sold for those engaged in the production of *mikote* (shea nut oil).

Table 4.4: The Intangible values of trees in Doko community

Sn	Plants native name	Scientific name	Cultural values				*count
			Medicine	Spiritual	Fruit	Shade	
1	Wuchi	Khaya Senegalensis	x				42
2	kulanchi	Crateva Adansonii	x	x			24
3	Goyiba	Psidium Guajava	x		x	x	22
4	Nambi sunsun	Crossopteryx febrifuge	x				18
5	Nimu	Azadirachta Indica	x			x	16
6	Kpache	Terminalia Schimperina	x				10
7	Konkeni	Carica Papaya	x		x		14
8	Lemu	Citrus	x		x	x	12
9	Yaba	Musa Sapientum	x		x		16
10	Mungoro	Mangifera Indica	x		x	x	12
11	Bafin	Pilostigma Thonningii	x	x			8
12	Gbashi	Sarcocephalus Latifolius	x	x			8
13	Gbanchi	Ficus Capensis	x			x	6
14	Zanchi kpara	Pterocarpus Erinaceus	x	x			6
15	Lonchi	Parkia Biglobosa	x	x	x	x	6
16	Eko	Butyrospermum indica	x		x	x	4
17	Danchi	Daniellia Oliveri	x				8
18	Jinjerechi	Spondias Mombin	x				4
19	Putu	Neocarya Macrophylla	x				4
20	Kukukpachi	Bombax Buonopozense	x				4
21	Sanchi	Prosopis Africana	x	x			4
22	Yikunu	Gutta percha tree			x		8

Spatially, within the community's cultural landscape, there exists a disparity between the number of species of trees found in the immediate vicinity of the compounds and those valued by the community members. The non-representativeness of medicinal and spiritual trees within the compound was explained by respondents with this statement:

"We fetch leaves, barks or roots of these trees once in a while, which lasts for some months and sometimes it could last us for a year."

Even though these medicinal trees are used by the community members, they do not need to have them within immediate reach since they could fetch enough to last them for some time. This is also reinforced by another respondent age 56, who gave the reasons for not having such medicinal trees domesticated in this anecdote:

"We go to farm every day and therefore we can fetch these medicines on our way back home"

This suggests that medicinal plants were not planted within the compounds because harvesting them was considered as part of the daily routine of going to the farm. Fruit trees are therefore domesticated while the cultural values of the non-fruit trees were derivable from their locations at the farms. Other sets of values associated with trees are the spiritual values. For example, a continuous quarrel between people could be diagnosed to have a spiritual undertone and thus curable. A family head affirms this in the following anecdote:

"My wives were very quarrelsome, but when I gave them bafin, their quarrel reduced"

The preparation of *bafin* condiment involves the use of seven leaves of *Pilostigma thonningii* which is plugged fresh and dried for seven days. The leaves are then ground and mixed with honey. The decoction is then shared into two portions and then individually given to the contending parties. Similarly, the nightmare is also a traditionally treatable ailment derivable from the use of trees. The bark of *saachi (Erythrophleum suaveolens)* is dried and grounded into powder and taken orally before going to bed. Furthermore, there are also species of trees which on their own do not constitute any medicinal values, but needs to be mixed with other condiments. This is further explained by a native respondent in this anecdote:

"We have these medicines called efoyikere, waka, tasubu, etun, and wasa; they are all made from the combination of different roots, leaves, and barks"

These traditional medicines are valued to have multiple functions. For example, *wasa* is on the one hand used for the treatment of snake bites, while on the other hand it is also used spiritually to prevent theft. The prevention of theft is constituted spiritually such that when a person attempts to steal an item protected with *wasa*, the person gets attacked by a snake. Similarly, *etun* is also made up of several different condiments of tree parts and it is believed by the Nupe community that the ingestion of *etun* does protect a person from natural hazards such as lightning and strikes of thunder.

Thunder and lightning strike are prevalent in the community and thus it is believed to be associated with evil spirits and therefore preventable. A person who takes *etun* is never struck by thunder. A person who gets struck is treated through the ingestion of the *etun* medicine. More about these derivatives of tree condiments with spiritual values are *tasubu* which, when ingested protects the person against evil forces. It is worth mentioning that deeper knowledge of these spiritual and intangible values of trees within the cultural landscape of Nupe communities is mostly in the confine of the native doctors. As such, most community members do consult the native doctors for the treatment of spiritual ailments.

Summarily, in the cultural landscapes of Doko community, the values of trees are constituted in both tangible and intangible forms. The tangible values of trees are associated with provision of shade and fruits. While the intangible values of trees were associated more with their spiritual values. Furthermore, the trees that constitute intangible values are found on the farms while trees with tangible values were located within the compounds.

Cultural values of water

Water forms an essential attribute for the sustenance of communities. Physical observations on the daily activities of the community show that for domestic use, the sources of water are wells, bore holes and the harvest of rainwater during raining seasons. The values associated with water are not limited to its use for biological needs, but also associated with more cultural values. This is seen the contextual mapping, illustrated in Figure 4.11.

A look at the "word tree" (Figure 4.11) shows that the value associated with water is multifaceted. For example, the statement made in one of the narrative states thus;

> *"Our boundary with Gaba is eyinkpata water."*

The meaning of water in the statement connotes river. In the cultural landscape of the Nupe community, water is the name given to most water related features such as streams, wells, and rivers. A further look at the statement also indicates that the river as a landscape feature is not just valued for its content, but also as a natural demarcation between the community and a neighbouring community. The value associated with water here is also in its function as a natural boundary demarcation for the community. This clearly gives an indication to all the community members to know when they are within their territory, such that they do not trespass into other community's property in activities such as farming and fishing.

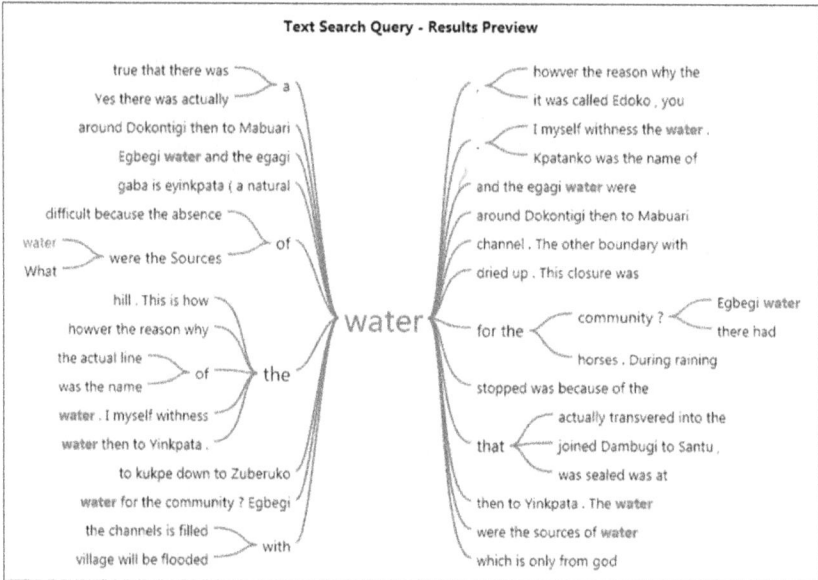

Text Search Query - Results Preview

Figure 4.11: The contextual word map of water

Conversely, while a water course served as a boundary between the community and neighbouring community. The gully, which transverses centrally through the community from the western side, is believed to be a water course which was sealed spiritually by the community's forefathers. The reason behind the closure of the water channel was to prevent it from being used as a transport route for slavery and inter-tribal wars prevalent during the early 18th century. It was also asserted that the channel was also a flood threat to the community. This is deduced contextually from the following three anecdotes:

"The reason why the water (river) was stopped was to prevent flood"

"Water was a flood threat to the community."

"Water was spiritually stopped and sealed at the base of the hill.."

The gully which transverse the community as shown in Figure 4.12 is believed to have been a river channel which was blocked spiritually by the community's forefathers.

Figure 4.12: The dried gully, supposedly an old river path

Even though the channel became dry, the community still recalls the memories of their forefathers, which prevented siege and flooding of the community. This forms an embodied value of people's transaction with their landscape (Mauricio, 2013). As such, in the cultural landscape, memory of the past and the symbolic representation of the gully results in the formation of an embodied value. When a landscape feature conveys meaning and also brings back historical events, then it has an additional dimension of enjoyment (Kim, 1988). As such, it can be stated that the waterscape of the Doko community is associated with multiple contextual meanings. Stolley (2005), relates this type of scenario to linguistics-relativity hypothesis which states that when something becomes central to the lives of people, it tends to take various forms of values and qualifications. Water in the community's cultural landscape is associated with values which are both tangible and intangible. The tangible values aside from the biological needs are associated with its meaning and value as a natural boundary delineator, while the intangible values are exemplified in the belief of the Nupes that the water body source was sealed spiritually by their forefathers which prevent the community from the flood.

Summary

This chapter showcased how culture influenced farming and farming related activities of a cultural landscape. Some of the highlights are the development of a cooperative system of farming called *dzoro*. Part of such cultural development is that the native people are able to have a good understanding and knowledge about their landscape towards the effective agricultural practices. Similarly, the continuous transactions with the landscape over a long period of time have resulted to local conceptualization of time, especially for farming activities. It therefore means that, cultural landscape transactions are culturally constitute to suit the economic as well as biological needs of the indigenous people.

Chapter 5

Indigenous Professions and Leadership Roles in Cultural Landscape Transactions

Operationalization of cultural landscape values

Cultural value in this book has been operationalized to be the social construct created from the cultural context of place and time. As such the values of a community are dependent on the landscape, the people and time. Similarly, cultural values are values shared by a community which is assessed through the perspectives of the people residing within the landscape. As such, cultural values assessment in this chapter discusses the tangible and the intangible values. Figure 5.1 summarily shows the nodes under each theme that formed the subject of discussion in this chapter.

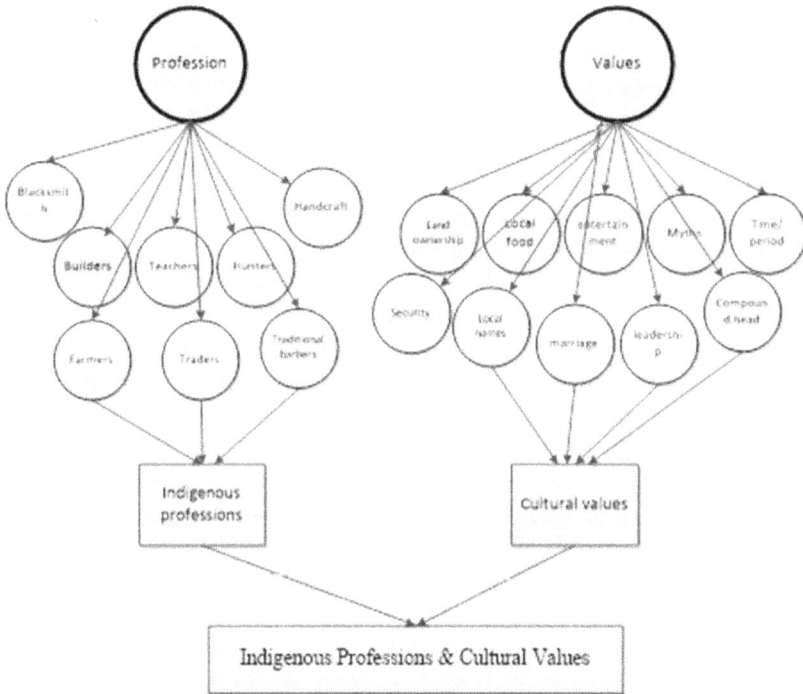

Figure 5.1: Indigenous profession transactions and cultural values relationship

Indigenous professions have an influence on the value system of each cultural landscape. However, these influences are constituted differently in each landscape. The analysis outputs of indigenous professions within the Nupe community in order of influence are farmers, traders and *gozan* for this section emphasis will be laid on farmers and traders besides, the transactions of *gozan* have already been discussed in Chapter 4.

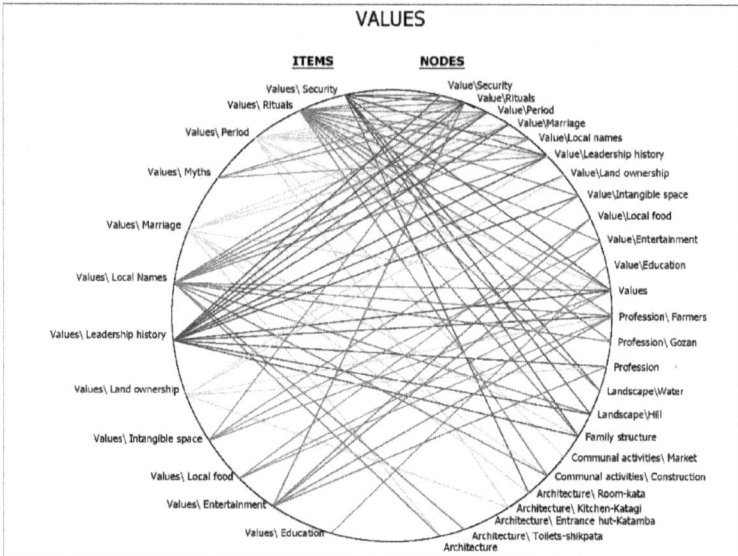

Figure 5.2: Nodes comparison query output for cultural values of Nupe community

As such the values of the Nupe community are embedded in the intersections of leadership, history, rituals, local names, security, marriages and time concepts with the major professions in the Nupe community.

Leadership history and cultural values

The social functioning of communities relies on leadership, Leadership system and structure that have links to the history of communities. The historical narratives from respondents ascribe the leadership to have started from the conglomeration of two clans of Edoko and Dazhi who sought to settle on the hill for refuge. The period of settlement on the hill can be traced down to the period of inter-tribal wars of early 18th century (Baikie and Kirk, 1867). History also shows that as at 1830's there was also the leadership struggle between the indigenous Nupe people and the Fulani tribe (Mason, 1975; Sarki, 2010). In the light of these, the two clans left their separate locations of settlement some kilometres away from the northeastern side of the hill and decided to merge and settle at on the hill. The anecdote from a respondent age 85, affirmed this as follows:

"Edoko people were the first to settle at the hillside and later on the Dazhi people came with their families.

The *Edoko* clan had settled first before a family of two brothers came to settle together with the Edoko community. During the course of staying together, there arose the need for the community to establish and select a leader to steer the affairs of the community. The anecdotes from two native respondents explain further:

"The Edoko people are originally hunters and thus did not want to be tied down to the sedentary life of leadership thus they asked the Dazhi clan who were then farmers to take the leadership"

"The Dazhi decided that he shall consult with his senior brother who settled at Kopa village before he would accept the leadership"

The narrations highlight several factors; first, the community of *Edoko* were mainly hunters, while the *Dazhi* clan were farmers. In terms of population, the *Edoko* clan had more people while the family of the *Dazhi* was made up of a single family.

The *Dazhi* consulted with his senior brother who gave him his blessing and thus asked that when it was time for the harvest of the bulrush millet, he should come over together with his people for the harvest. Respondent aged 86 further elaborates:

Kopa village had a fertile soil so the harvest there was good. That is why even up to today the Dazhi people go to Kopa for the annual fishing called ewon.

Thus, this marked the beginning of the symbolic event of harvest in a neighbouring community 4 kilometres south-west of Doko. This inter-village relationship of the annual harvest of bulrush millet has stopped. The reason would not be too far-fetched in the sense that Doko people are now also into full farming and thus harvesting of bulrush millet from a smaller village would not be of much economic value both to the leadership and the entire population. However, the symbolic act in which the two communities come together annually is still practiced in another form called *ewon*. *Ewon* is a large depression located along the flood channels and it thus forms an annual collection pool for fish. The two communities towards the end of each dry season, when the floods have receded converge to fish at the designated location. The value of this annual event called *ewon* which symbolizes the historic choice of a leader continues to contribute to the intangible values of unity between the two communities.

Furthermore, going back to the selection of the leader, the *Edoko* people gave up the leadership to a smaller clan. Even though the Edoko clan had a leader named *Zhitsu bebi*, the leadership of the entire community was relinquished to the *Dazhi* clan because it was then seen to hinder the pursuit of their profession which was hunting. As such the leadership of the community continues to be in the lineage of the smaller *Dazhi* clan. Contrastingly, when compared to other communities, the ascendance into leadership by later settler occurred mostly through force. Such examples are demonstrated in the ascendance into leadership in neighbouring Nupe communities of Nupeko by Tsoede in 1531 and the Fulani leadership of Mallam Dendo in Bida town in 1831 (Idrees, 1998; Mason, 1975). However, the Doko community relinquished their leadership voluntarily. More also is the possibility that the dominance of a particular clan could force a peaceful selection of leadership from a larger group. However, in the case of Doko community, the ruling class did not emerge from the large clan of *Edoko* but rather from a single family of *Dazhi*.

Over time, the profession of the Edoko people changed from hunting to full fledge subsistence farming. However, by then the *Dazhi* leadership had established the control of most of the farmlands. The anecdote from a respondent aged 85 shows the effect of the decision taken by the forefathers in the leadership of the community.

> "Our Ndako (forefather) never knew that this is how it would be, they wouldn't have given the leadership to the Dazhi family. The Edoko people were more and are still more in number today. The Edoko people were engrossed in the old tradition of honouring the visitors and thus they left the leadership to the visitors"

The statement from the respondent shows some inkling of regrets from the decisions of the founding fathers of the community who had the opportunity of leading the community, but decided to give it out to the smaller clan and also later settlers. Despite this, the community continues to honour the decision of the forefathers such that status quo is maintained. The leadership of *Dazhi* and the historic values associated with the choice of *Dazhi* leadership continues to influence and shape the values of all land related activities in Doko community.

Farmland transactions and the influence leadership

The economics of rural communities in Africa is underpinned with the utilization of the farm lands and its resources for the satisfaction of the needs of the community. Similarly, subsistence farming constitutes the main profession of Nupe communities and also constitutes the source of their economic well-being. Generally, the acquisition of land in Nigeria is ascribed to be the properties of the central government. However, in Doko community, the land is administered by the *Dazhi*, the village head. In the terminology of the natives, *Etsu Dazhi ga wun kin yan o*, which means *Dazhi* owns the land. As such the Dazhi is the main custodian of farmlands in Doko community. Exceptions, however, exist in some instances as some council members and also compound heads are allowed control of a certain parcel of land. For example, *bana* farm located about 2 kilometres on the western side of the community is in the control of *Ndalagba* the compound head of *Emilangba* household. However, the Dazhi by right of his position could influence a decision on these farms if he picks an interest in them.

Furthermore, the position of the leadership places the *Dazhi* on some economic benefits from each farmer's annual harvest which is called *eyan-kin* (land tax). *Eyan-kin* is paid on a pro rata basis, such that what the *Dazhi* gets is calculated proportionally to the quantity of each farmer's harvest. The crop that generates more *eyan-kin* is rice because it is the main economic crop of the community while other crops such as the guinea corn maize and tubers are mostly cultivated in smaller scales for individual family domestic consumptions.

In another perspective, the *Dazhi* also benefits from free labour on his farm which in the local dialect is called *egbe*. Here a call is made from time to time for the community members, especially the youth, to voluntarily work on the *Dazhi* farms. As such the availability of large volunteer workforce avails the leadership with the economic values to cultivate larger farms than any other person in the community.

Surmising the economics of leadership and farming in the cultural landscape of Doko community, it can be deduced that the cultural land tenure system places the leadership on a higher pedestal of economic benefits compared to the rest of the populace. The foregoing showcases the role of the general populace and their contribution to the economic well-being of the leadership. The next section discusses the transactions of typical farmers within the Nupe community.

Transactions of Farmers

Most farmers in the Nupe community cultivate different variety of crops which are also located on different plots. These plots could be of considerable distances of several kilometres away from each other, an anecdotal from a native farmer affirms this as follows:

> *"lati yan bana rogo mi yan nun bo o,*
> *lati yan yeka guza mi yan nun bo o,*
> *lati yan kantifigi epin be eyi mi yan nun bo o,*
> *lati yan sondogi chekafa mi yan nun bo o"*

This means

> *"I cultivate cassava on my bana farm*
> *I cultivate ground nut on my yeka farm*
> *I cultivate melon and guinea corn on my farm at kantifigi and*
> *I cultivate rice on my farm located at sondogi"*

From the narrations, *Bana, Yeka, Kantififigi* and *Sondongi* are farm plots located at different routes and directions. Modern economics of farming would have suggested that a farmer should have a large plot of land, such that the plots are partitioned into segments to cultivate different crops within the same plot (mixed cropping). The argument that will arise is that in terms of transportation and ease of monitoring the use of one large plot of farmland as against several plots situated in different locations would be more advantageous. However, for the local farmer, the reverse is the case as seen in this anecdote

> *"Kin dodo de yangichi na we geya nao"*

The literal translation means;

> *"Each location has a designated crop that thrives better on it."*

This means that for the Nupe farmer, each location has what is most suitable to be cultivated since they are engaged in the cultivation of varieties of crops. As such, over time, the Nupe farmer has been able to acquire a traditional ecological knowledge of their landscape. However, it is common to find the same type of crops planted by different farmers in the same location. In this situation for an outside observer, several plots will look as if it belongs to one person because there exists no physical barrier between different farms; more also that the crops are usually planted almost at the same period. One would, therefore, think that boundary disputes may arise. However, two respondents suggest otherwise on why such disputes hardly occur.

"egwa gbara yan zandon doa kperi",

Which means, the ridge signature of each farmer is different"

"Ena zan don do ga nuna ga wun gbe o o"

Which means what each farmer cultivate is what he will reap"

The community still practices manual hoe agriculture system of farming and thus from this, it suggests that each farmer pattern of ridges differs in terms of size and thus it distinctively stands out from one another. Furthermore, in the making of the ridges, farmers do make them in a different direction, such that the ridges of one plot could run perpendicular to a neighbour's plot.

The second respondents' comments on each farmer reaping what he sows indicates that, since the whole farm plots belong to the *Dazhi,* there was no need for boundary disputes. More also is the fact that, what is important to the farmer is not the plot itself, but rather the effort of the cultivation which is clearly identified by the annual ridges formation signature. Thus, for the general population of farmers, the value of the leadership is portrayed in an intangible form. This is because, the position of the *Dazhi* as the custodian of farm plots prevent disputes, especially as regards to farm boundaries because the natives concentrate on the product of their cultivation rather than the plots.

Market scene as a gendered place

Trading as a profession in the cultural landscape of the Nupe community as mentioned in chapter 4 is the realm of Nupe women. To rephrase, the role of the women folk in the economics of the community is in the processing of the farm products and its sales in the market. Thus, this clearly makes areas of expertise to be gender specific within the cultural landscape of the community. This is because; the farm activity is dominated by the male folks while the market landscape is dominated by the female folks as illustrated Figure 5.3 and 5.4.

One fact worth mentioning is that even though the market scene is dominated by the womenfolk, the leader of the market is a male person. The male leadership is called *Etsu Dzuko*, the market chief. This could be as a result of the ease with which the *Etsu dzuko* can blend with the male-dominated village council. The leadership of the *Etsu dzuko* is not limited to the economics of revenue generation, but also extends to the wellbeing of the people in the market. A 35-year-old female respondent asserts the following:

> *"The Etsu dzuko settles disputes between market women, he ensures the meat, and the grain and even the market is kept clean. He can even detect and also ensures that anyone with evil intent is not allowed into the market."*

As such, in the market scene, the *Etsu dzuko* plays multiple roles of being a sanitary inspector, an arbitrator of disputes, a police officer, spiritual leader and an administrator. Summarily, the traditional professions in the cultural landscape community are uniquely practiced such that multiple skills abound within a single profession. Similarly, all indigenous professional practice is linked to the leadership at the centre in the person of *Dazhi*, the community leader.

Figure 5.3: The sugar cane section of the market

Figure 5.4: The vegetable section of the market

Chapter 6

Overview of Tangible and Intangible Cultural Values of Nupe Community

This research sets out to determine the cultural landscape value of a Nupe community in north central Nigeria. The cultural landscape was set on the premise of the everyday environment of the local people in which they transact for their daily living. Value was considered in both tangible and intangible forms so long as it made meaning to the people who inhabit the landscape. The scale of the transaction was set within the boundary in which the local people interact to meet their daily needs. Therefore, the research laid emphasis on the Nupe people's perspectives, their world views and what their landscape means to them.

There existed numerous cultural landscape transactions in the Nupe community. As such a claim that all aspects of such transactions have been covered in this book will be false. However, the study ensured that despite its exploratory nature, some frameworks guided the elicitations of information; this is to ensure that the basic spatial transactions of people are covered in the study. Firstly, the Habitat Theory, which stipulates that people transact with the environment in order to satisfy their biological needs constituted a primary base of data elicitations. Secondly, the Prospect and Refuge Theory, which asserts that people and each community are constituted based on the balance of prospect and refuge forces was also employed to enrich the inquiry process. Notwithstanding this, the uniqueness of Nupe cultural landscape transaction was allowed to emerge naturally starting with the domestic space transactions.

Cultural values of domestic space

The system of living within Nupe community is established on an extended family system and this is reflected spatially. The layout of the compound is made such that individual families are spatially constituted in separate courtyards which are connected through alleys to form a compound. The family structure of the Nupe community is established more on the *efako* system of living. *Efako* is a family system which is established based on the collective work on the farm. The *efako* family system of the Nupe is made up of both biological and non-biological members such as adopted children. The uniqueness of the Nupe family system is exemplified in the rights which adopted children have in leadership as well as the inheritance of land. Contrastingly, the womenfolk in the *efako* system are not considered in their paternal homes in terms of spatial allocations. Rather, the Nupe cultural norm is that women belong to their spouse's house. This has a spatial implication because; the physical development of the compound is centred more for the provision of accommodation for the male children. However, while on the one hand women are not included in the provision of permanent space their father's house; they are on the other hand, given more priority in their spouse's house in terms of spatial considerations. Some of the cultural norms are that it is a prerequisite for a bedroom to be built for the bride before a marriage is conducted. Furthermore, the control of the domestic space is more with the women rather than the men in the daily transactions of the family.

The most compelling evidence of women's control of the domestic space is that they dominate in the spatial transactions of the bedroom and the courtyard. Several transactions occur within the courtyard space by the women folk amongst which is cooking. The cooking space of the Nupe woman is of two types, the *nanche* (the open kitchen), and the *katagi* (the covered kitchen). The propensity to use is more in the open kitchen which is located within the courtyard and the covered kitchen only becomes useful when the weather does not allow such as rainfall.

On the other hand, the male spatial transactions mostly occur at the entrance hall and its surrounding. It, therefore, means that a person needs to pass through the male-dominated areas first before getting to the female dominated area. The spatial transactions of the children, male and the female members of the family are illustrated in Figure 6.1.

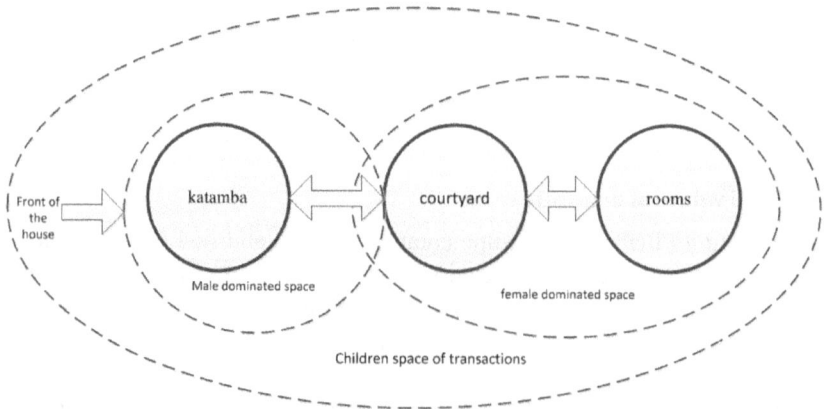

Figure 6.1: The spatial transactions of the Nupe family within the domestic space

The *katamba* (entrance hall) in Nupe compounds constitutes an important architectural feature within the domestic space. In the first place, the *katamba* symbolically marks the entrance to the compound as well as the men's place of congregation for meetings and relaxation. As such, the front of the compounds, where the *katamba* is situated mostly has fruit trees planted to provide fruits and shade. The fruits are mostly the orange and mango. A few compounds have two *katamba*, front, and back.

It is worth mentioning that the value of the *katamba* transcends beyond its use as space to also include its use as a geographic reference to the whole compound as illustrated in Figure 6.2.

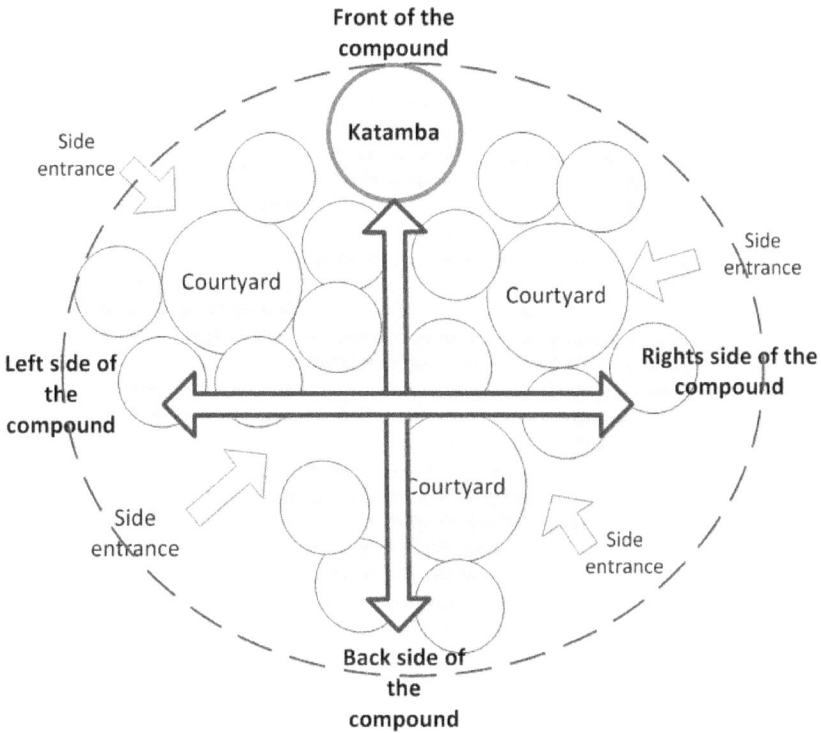

Front of the
compound

Katamba

Side
entrance

Side
entrance

Courtyard

Courtyard

Left side of
the
compound

Rights side of the
compound

Courtyard

Side
entrance

Side
entrance

Back side of
the
compound

Figure 6.2: The katamba as a geographic reference point for a Nupe compound

The use of *katamba* as a geographic reference point is of high intangible cultural value due to one major factor. The Nupe compounds have several courtyards occupied by individual families as such several entrances other than the *katamba* are found. As such, the Nupes use the location of the *katamba* as the front and it is from it that the other sides of the house (left, right and back) take their references.

Each cultural landscape is established with professions that sustain the needs of the people. In Nupe communities, the main traditional professions are farming, *gozan* (local barbers-doctor) and the traders. These professions transact within the community and in the course of such transactions, the landscape features are found to contribute towards their practices. For example, within the Nupe community, water bodies, the market space and the hill are found to play some significant role. The market, which is the place for commercial transactions, is located within the core of the community. The placement of the market within the Centre is a cultural norm which gives all people a sense of equal connection. Such connectedness is exemplified in the approximate equal distance of access from different locations. Similarly, also is the equal opportunity of visual connection to the center. This thus showcases a planning concept that enhances a sense of collectivism and sense of spatial belonging to public spaces.

Women within the cultural landscape play their professional roles as traders. In their transactions, two key landscape features, water, and the hill are of high cultural value. The importance of water transcends beyond its use for domestic chores to include its use for the processing of farm products. As such, each compound has at least a well for water supply. It is to be noted that the most important crop of Nupe community is rice and before it gets to the market water from the wells and the stream are the sources for the washing and parboiling. Similarly, the hill serves as the source of firewood for the parboiling of rice. In the light of this, the landscape features of water and the hill are of cultural value to the trader's (women) and the community's economic wellbeing.

The market space has a more direct value relationship with the women who are by cultural default the traders of the community. However, the farmers who are the males have indirect cultural values because the transactions of the female folk at the market are mostly farm produce, the product of the male folks. In the light of this, the women invariably are the financial managers. The women's continuous engagement with the activities of market transactions ensures that security of cash flow is established. In doing so, the community is kept afloat with cash, which men access readily for the purchase of farm inputs.

The cultural value of this profession of the women is also reinforced by the presence of the community leadership through the *Etsu Dzuko*. Even though the market is dominated by the females, the *Etsu Dzuko* position is occupied by the men. He serves as the link between the women dominated transactions of the market and the male-dominated village council.

Conceptualization of time

Activities of Nupe communities are tied to the sequence of farming and landscape indicators. The Nupe community does not necessarily use the universal concept of time rather the landscape tells time. These landscape indicators are constituted in different forms such as the appearance of *mani-mani* insects which mark the beginning of the raining season. The disappearance of monkeys from the immediate landscape marks the end of the cropping season. The sequence in which crops mature and are harvested also gives some cultural time indicators such as the harvest of bulrush millet, which matures and gets harvested after forty days to pave the way for the sowing of groundnut and sweet potatoes. However, in the flood plains, the time for cultivation depends on the level of flood. As such the Nupe people have an established knowledge of predicting the time in which plots of lands on the flood plains are to be cultivated. Furthermore, when the flood comes, the local people are able to control it for an effective farming activity. This suggests an established traditional ecological knowledge of the Nupe people about their landscape.

Equally important is that farming provides security, in terms of food and sustains the community's social institution of marriage from the output. It also portrays the community's cultural values of leadership system through *Dazhi* land ownership and control. Similarly, the *gozan* (barber-doctor) constitutes some cultural values which are in both tangible and intangible forms. The tangible forms are portrayed in the performance of the annual rituals of *wasa* performance, and the daily services they offer through shaving of the head and circumcisions, while the intangible values are constituted in the provision of security against natural and spiritual forces. Furthermore, the conduct of an annual ritual within a specific un-built space showcases the development of an intangible architecture, an architecture that exists without any structure being built.

All things considered, the Nupe community cultural landscape is such that the professions of the people are uniquely characterised based on culture and the character of the landscape. In Nupe community landscape, the constituents of leadership, security, performance of traditional rituals, and the concept of time are subsumed within the transactions of the farmers, the *gozan*, and the traders. This thus culminates into categorical statements that can be made to define the cultural landscape values of Nupe community. These categorical statements are hereby referred to as the grounded theory.

The grounded theory of Nupe cultural landscape

The grounded theory is a series of statements made which are grounded on data gathered from the field to define a phenomena. As such, in concluding this book, the followings are the Grounded theory about the Nupe community.

    i.   Three spaces are the most important features of domestic landscape transactions; they are the female dominated spaces of the courtyard, the bedroom and the male-dominated area of the *katamba*.

ii.   The most important plants within the domestic space are the fruit providing species of trees.

iii.   The farmers, the *gozan,* and the traders are the most important profession of the community cultural landscape and thus define and shapes the values the Nupe people in the use of spaces

iv.   Transactions of Doko community are tied to local time concepts which are defined by the sequence of farm activities

v.   The professions of the Nupe community are gender specific such that the men are the farmers and the women are the traders.

vi.   The landscape features which define the values of the community are the hill, fruit trees and water.

vii.   The Nupe community transactions are tied to the leadership of *Dazhi* thus constitutes a sense of collectivism.

Summarily, the grounded theory about the Nupe community is graphically represented in Figure 6.3.

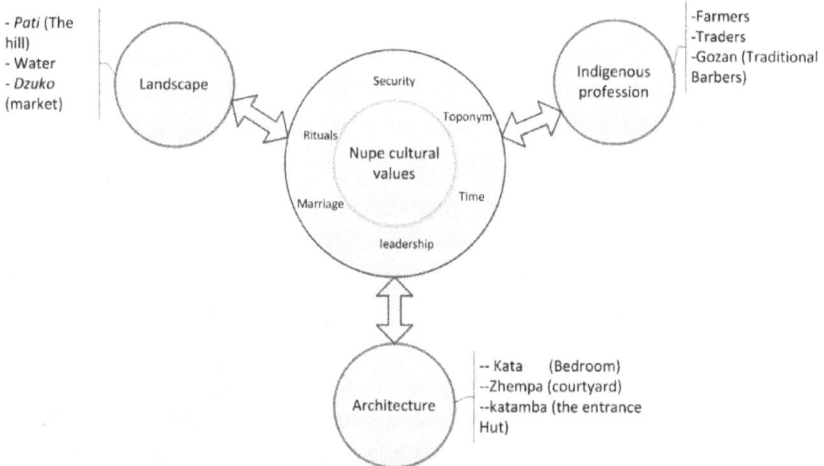

Figure 6.3: The graphic representation of the grounded theory of Nupe Community

Figure 6.3, on the one hand, illustrated the bi-directional influences of indigenous architecture, landscape, and professions on the values of the community. On the other hand, the values of the community also shape the individual features of architecture professions and landscape.

Design implications

To accommodate a typical Nupe man, the house must have a katamba and an open space of at least fifty percent of the built-up area. In the terminology of the Nupe community, *emi*, is home and it is thus made up of several families living within a common boundary with a katamba which serve as a symbolic common entrance and a place for the reception of guests of the family. Furthermore, the Nupe home design is expected to have a minimum of 50 percent of the compound space left open as a courtyard. Equally important in the Nupe compound layout is to allow visual contact with the outside and also prevent the infiltrations of external view into the private views of the rooms. Thus, one directional visual contact is to be made through the use of the local blind *shegi*. The importance of the traditional blind *shegi* aside from its functions in the visual connections and disconnection is that it also forms an effective means for the lighting of the rooms and also cross ventilations. This concept of *shegi* blind could also be extended to apply in contemporary designs to suit other hot climatic conditions. Furthermore, the Nupe traditional concept of layout also suggests that visual connections can provide security within a build up space without necessarily building of physical barriers.

Planning and policy implication

The cultural landscape is about peoples' perspectives and the world as perceived by them and doing so would allow government understand and implement policies that are sustainable for both the community and the government itself. Recently, there has been some advocacy on how the ecosystem can be protected and preserved. Since each culture has what it values, it can, therefore, be stated that within the purview of the Nupe cultural landscapes the medicinal plants which are made up of several species of trees in the wild stand a good chance of being preserved. As such, the planting of culturally valued species of trees becomes more sustainable. Furthermore, the establishment of policies about the Nupe community has a strong chance of acceptance when the community is engaged through its leadership of *Dazhi*. While in afforestation policies of the government, fruit producing trees are more likely to be protected within the community domestic space and the spiritually valued trees in the wild.

Theoretical implications

It is the conviction of the researcher that the study of the cultural landscape, especially about a minority ethnic group of Nupe in Nigeria is first of its kind. As such it opens up a pedestal for scholars to engage in understanding the Nupe people's perceptions about their cultural landscape. Furthermore, ethnography in cultural landscape studies as employed in this research gives more credence to understanding the cultural landscape. Therefore, the methods are not only limited to Nupe cultural landscape, but could transcend into understanding other cultural landscapes.

Conclusion

The research affirms that the cultural landscape transactions are uniquely characterised. The cultural value of each community differs and portrayed in different forms. Some of which are the uniqueness of the family system of the Nupe community which is established on *efako*. A family system based on the collective work on the farm rather than biological relationship. The landscape feature of the hill whose values are not tied to its physicality but rather more on the memories it holds of being the first place where the community sought refuge.

Likewise, in the domestic space, the courtyard of the Nupe compound is not limited to the bioclimatic function alone. Rather the cultural values of the courtyard include its use as a space for domestic chores, a sleeping space and its intangible function of visual connections to the surrounding landscape of the hill. Similarly, the transactions of the Nupe community do not rely on the global time concept, but to the series and sequence of events tied to farming and special events of the community. Thus, the Nupe people depend on event time rather than the clock time.

In the same manner, the Nupe woman continues to maintain the culture where enamelled bowls are used in place of pots to decorate the rooms. It thus suggests that in the cultural lives of people, change of material may not necessarily mean a change in concepts, but rather an adaptation of the new material to suit the cultural lifestyle of the people.

Additionally, the discussion of the Nupe people portrays their inclinations towards collectivism rather than individualistic tendencies. This is demonstrated in the community through the representation of all the compounds in the village council where decisions are collectively carried out. Equally important in the transactions of the community is the concepts of provision of security without the use of physical barriers. Instead, spaces are left open to have visual connections. Consequently, the cultural landscape values of the Nupe community are uniquely shaped by their culture and the landscape.

References

Adegbija, E. (2004). Language Policy and Planning in Nigeria. *Current Issues in Language Planning*. 5(3), 181-246.

Aldous, J. (1962). Urbanization, the extended family, and kinship ties in West Africa. *Social Forces*. 41(1), 6-12.

Anderson, N. M., Williams, K. J. and Ford, R. M. (2013). Community perceptions of plantation forestry: The association between place meanings and social representations of a contentious rural land use. *Journal of Environmental Psychology*. 34, 121-136.

Antrop, M. (1997). The concept of traditional landscapes as a base for landscape evaluation and planning. The example of Flanders Region. *Landscape and urban planning*. 38(1), 105-117.

Appleton, J. (1975). *The experience of landscape*. London, Beccles and Colchester: John Wiley and Sons Ltd.

Bal, M.-C., Allée, P. and Liard, M. (2015). The origins of a Nardus stricta grassland through soil charcoal analyses: Reconstructing the history of a mountain cultural landscape (Mont Lozère, France) since the Neolithic. *Quaternary International*. 366, 3-14.

Bennardo, G. (2009). *Language, space, and social relationships: A foundational cultural model in Polynesia*. Cambridge University Press.

Bergeron, J., Paquette, S. and Poullaouec-Gonidec, P. (2014). Uncovering landscape values and micro-geographies of meanings with the go-along method. *Landscape and Urban Planning*. 122, 108-121.

Biglu, M.-H., Farnam, A., Abotalebi, P., Biglu, S. and Ghavami, M. (2016). Effect of female genital mutilation/cutting on sexual functions. *Sexual & Reproductive Healthcare*. http://dx.doi.org/10.1016/j.srhc.2016.07.002.

Biklen, S. (2010). The quality of evidence in qualitative research. *International Encyclopedia of Education*. 488-497.

Bokova, I. (2015). Culture on the Front Line of New Wars. *Brown J. World Aff*. 22, 289.

Cieraad, I. (2006). *At home: an anthropology of domestic space*. Syracuse University Press.

Coontz, S. (2000). Historical perspectives on family studies. *Journal of marriage and family*. 62(2), 283-297.

Cotton, W. R., Bryan, G. and van den Heever, S. C. (2011). The Influence of Mountains on Airflow, Clouds, and Precipitation. *International Geophysics*. 99, 673-750.

Cullotta, S. and Barbera, G. (2011). Mapping traditional cultural landscapes in the Mediterranean area using a combined multidisciplinary approach: Method and application to Mount Etna (Sicily; Italy). *Landscape and Urban Planning*. 100(1), 98-108.

De, A. (2016). Spatialisation of selves: Religion and liveable spaces among Hindus and Muslims in the walled city of Ahmedabad, India. *City, Culture and Society*. 7(3), 149-154.

del Barrio, M. J., Devesa, M. and Herrero, L. C. (2012). Evaluating intangible cultural heritage: The case of cultural festivals. *City, Culture and Society.* 3(4), 235-244.

Donovan, K. and Gkartzios, M. (2014). Architecture and rural planning: 'Claiming the vernacular'. *Land Use Policy.* 41, 334-343.

Draper, P. (1989). African marriage systems: Perspectives from evolutionary ecology. *Ethology and Sociobiology.* 10(1-3), 145-169.

Drozdzewski, D. (2014). Using history in the streetscape to affirm geopolitics of memory. *Political Geography.* 42, 66-78.

Dzanku, F. M. (2015). Transient rural livelihoods and poverty in Ghana. *Journal of Rural Studies.* 40, 102-110.

ELC (2012). European Landscape Convention, Treaty series. In 2012, P. t. P. b. t. S. o. S. f. F. a. C. A. b. C. o. H. M. J. (Ed.).

Glaser, B. G. and Strauss, A. L. (2009). *The discovery of grounded theory: Strategies for qualitative research.* Transaction Publishers.

Gullino, P. and Larcher, F. (2012). Integrity in UNESCO World Heritage Sites. A comparative study for rural landscapes. *Journal of Cultural Heritage.* http://dx.doi.org/10.1016/j.culher.2012.10.005.

Gunner, L. (2005). Remapping land and remaking culture: memory and landscape in 20th-century South Africa. *Journal of Historical Geography.* 31(2), 281-295.

Hermann, A., Kuttner, M., Hainz-Renetzeder, C., Konkoly-Gyuró, É., Tirászi, Á., Brandenburg, C., Allex, B., Ziener, K. and Wrbka, T. (2014). Assessment framework for landscape services in European cultural landscapes: an Austrian Hungarian case study. *Ecological indicators.* 37, 229-240.

Hillier, B., Hanson, J. and Graham, H. (1987). Ideas are in things: an application of the space syntax method to discovering house genotypes. *Environment and Planning B: planning and design.* 14(4), 363-385.

House, W. (2010). Heritage Impact Assessment of Construction and Upgrading of Ingquza Hill to Mangwanini Access Roads, Flagstaff, Eastern Cape Province, South Africa.

Howley, P., Donoghue, C. O. and Hynes, S. (2012). Exploring public preferences for traditional farming landscapes. *Landscape and Urban Planning.* 104(1), 66-74.

Idrees, A. (1998). Political Change and Continuity in Nupeland. *Caltop Pub.(Nig.) Ltd. Ibadan Nigeria.* 1-14.

Jones, M. (2007). The European Landscape Convention and the question of public participation. *Landscape Research.* 32(5), 613-633.

Kent, S. (1993). Activity areas and architecture: an interdisciplinary view or the relationship between use or space and domestic built environments. In Kent, S. (Ed.) *Domestic architecture and the use of space: an interdisciplinary cross-cultural study*
(pp. 1-8). Australia: Cambridge University Press.

Kim, S.-K. (1988). *Winding river village: poetics of a Korean landscape,* University of Pennsylvania.

Lemelin, R. H., Koster, R. and Youroukos, N. (2015). Tangible and intangible indicators of successful aboriginal tourism initiatives: A case study of two successful aboriginal tourism lodges in Northern Canada. *Tourism Management*. 47, 318-328.

Linehan, J. R. and Gross, M. (1998). Back to the future, back to basics: the social ecology of landscapes and the future of landscape planning. *Landscape and Urban Planning*. 42(2), 207-223.

Maina, J. J. (2013). Uncomfortable prototypes: Rethinking socio-cultural factors for the design of public housing in Billiri, north east Nigeria. *Frontiers of Architectural Research*. 2(3), 310-321.

Mann, A. and Ogbadoyi, E. O. (2012). Evaluation of medicinal plants from Nupeland for their in vivo antitrypanosomal activity. *American Journal of Biochemistry*. 2(1), 1-6.

Martin, T. F. (2015). Advancing dynamic family theories: Applying optimal matching analysis to family research. *Journal of Family Theory & Review*. 7(4), 482-497.

Mauricio, H. B. (2013). The significance and meanings of public space improvement in low-income neighbourhoods, colonias populares' in Xalapa-Mexico. *Habitat International*. 38, 34-46.

Meekers, D. (1992). The process of marriage in African societies: A multiple indicator approach. *Population and development review*. 61-78.

Muhammad-Oumar, A. A. (1997). *Gidaje: The socio-cultural morphology of Hausa living Spaces*, University of London.

Muhammad, I. B. and Said, I. (2015a). Behavioral use of courtyard in a Nupe cultural landscape of Nigeria. *Proceedings of the 2015 Interdisciplinary Behavior and Social Sciences: Proceedings of the International Congress on Interdisciplinary Behaviour and Social Sciences 2014*: CRC Press, 227.

Muhammad, I. B. and Said, I. (2015b). Spatial Transactions and Vernacular Architecture of a Nupe Community in Central Nigeria. *Jurnal Teknologi*. 77(15), 1-7.

Muhammad, I. B. and Said, I. B. (2014). Cultural landscape value and spatial representation of trees in a rural Nupe community of Nigeria. *Proceedings of the 2014 International Alliance for Sustainable Urbanization and regeneration* 24-27 October 2014. Kashiwa Japan, 272-280.

Muller, L. (2008). Intangible and tangible landscapes: an anthropological perspective based on two South African case studies.

Musa, S. (2004). The impact of the Sokoto jihad on Nupeland *Proceedings of the 2004 2004 International Seminar on The Bicentenary Of The Sokoto Caliphate 1804-2004*. 14th to 16th June. Abuja, Nigeria

Nadel, S. F. (1942). *A black Byzantium: the kingdom of Nupe in Nigeria*. International Institute of African languages & cultures.

Nasongkhla, S. (2010). Tai-Lanna-Shan Cultural Landscapes Reproduction of Identity. *Proceedings of the 2010 International Symposium: Identity of Traditional Asian landscape* National university, Seoul, Korea. 81-96.

Niță, A., Buttler, A., Rozylowicz, L. and Pătru-Stupariu, I. (2015). Perception and use of landscape concepts in the procedure of Environmental Impact Assessment: Case study—Switzerland and Romania. *Land Use Policy*. 44, 145-152.

NPC (2006) *Nigeria Population Census Report, (NPC 2006)*. Abuja.

Nunta, J. and Sahachaisaeree, N. (2010). Determinant of cultural heritage on the spatial setting of cultural landscape: a case study on the northern region of Thailand. *Procedia-Social and Behavioral Sciences.* 5, 1241-1245.

Nwanodi, O. B. A. (1989). Hausa compounds: Products of cultural, economic, social and political systems. *Habitat International.* 13(4), 83-97.

O'Reilly, K. (2009). *Key concepts in ethnography.* London: SAGE Publications Limited.

Ódor, P., Király, I., Tinya, F., Bortignon, F. and Nascimbene, J. (2014). Reprint of: Patterns and drivers of species composition of epiphytic bryophytes and lichens in managed temperate forests. *Forest Ecology and Management.* 321(0), 42-51.

Palang, H., Alumäe, H., Printsmann, A., Rehema, M., Sepp, K. and Sooväli-Sepping, H. (2011). Social landscape: Ten years of planning 'valuable landscapes' in Estonia. *Land Use Policy.* 28(1), 19-25.

Parsaee, M., Parva, M. and Karimi, B. (2014). Space and place concepts analysis based on semiology approach in residential architecture: The case study of traditional city of Bushehr, Iran. *HBRC Journal.*

Pellow, D. (2003). The architecture of female seclusion in West Africa. *The anthropology of space and place: Locating culture. Blackwell readers in anthropology. Malden: Blackwell Publishers.*

Price, J. C., Walker, I. A. and Boschetti, F. (2014). Measuring cultural values and beliefs about environment to identify their role in climate change responses. *Journal of Environmental Psychology.* 37, 8-20.

Prussin, L. (1974). An introduction to indigenous African architecture. *Journal of the Society of Architectural Historians.* 33(3), 183-205.

Ramírez, Á., Ayuga-Téllez, E., Gallego, E., Fuentes, J. M. and García, A. I. (2011). A simplified model to assess landscape quality from rural roads in Spain. *Agriculture, ecosystems & environment.* 142(3), 205-212.

Rapoport, A. (1969). House form and culture. Foundations of cultural geography series. *Englewood Cliffs, New Jersey.*

Rapoport, A. (1993). Systems of activities and systems of settings. In Kent, S. (Ed.) *Domestic architecture and the use of space: an interdisciplinary cross-cultural study*

(pp. 9-20). Melbourne, Australia: Cambridge University Press.

Risjord, M. (2007). Ethnography and culture. In P. S. (Ed.) *Handbook of the Philosophy of Science. Philosophy of Anthropology and Sociology* (pp. 399-428) Elsevier B.V.

Róin, Á. (2015). The multifaceted notion of home: Exploring the meaning of home among elderly people living in the Faroe Islands. *Journal of Rural Studies.* 39, 22-31.

Rössler, M. (2006). World heritage cultural landscapes: a UNESCO flagship programme 1992–2006. *Landscape Research.* 31(4), 333-353.

Sarki, S. U. (2010). *The making of Masaba dynasty.* Minna: Haligraph Nigeria Ltd.

Seamon, D. (2015). Situated cognition and the phenomenology of place: lifeworld, environmental embodiment, and immersion-in-world. *Cognitive processing.* 16(1), 389-392.

Stephenson, J. (2005). *Values in Space and Time: A frame work for Understanding and Linking Cultural Values in Landscapes.* Doctor of Philosophy, University of Otago, Dunedin, New Zealand.

Stephenson, J. (2008). The Cultural Values Model: An integrated approach to values in landscapes. *Landscape and urban planning.* 84(2), 127-139.

Stolley, K. S. (2005). *The basics of sociology.* Greenwood Publishing Group.

Taylor, J. J. (2008). Naming the land: San countermapping in Namibia's West Caprivi. *Geoforum.* 39(5), 1766-1775.

Tengberg, A., Fredholm, S., Eliasson, I., Knez, I., Saltzman, K. and Wetterberg, O. (2012). Cultural ecosystem services provided by landscapes: Assessment of heritage values and identity. *Ecosystem Services.*

Tian, Y., Jim, C. and Wang, H. (2014). Assessing the landscape and ecological quality of urban green spaces in a compact city. *Landscape and urban planning.* 121, 97-108.

Torquati, B., Giacchè, G. and Venanzi, S. (2015). Economic analysis of the traditional cultural vineyard landscapes in Italy. *Journal of Rural Studies.* 39, 122-132.

Turner, K. G., Odgaard, M. V., Bøcher, P. K., Dalgaard, T. and Svenning, J.-C. (2014). Bundling ecosystem services in Denmark: Trade-offs and synergies in a cultural landscape. *Landscape and Urban Planning.* 125, 89-104.

Ujang, N. and Zakariya, K. (2015). The Notion of Place, Place Meaning and Identity in Urban Regeneration. *Procedia-Social and Behavioral Sciences.* 170, 709-717.

Van Eetvelde, V. and Antrop, M. (2009). Indicators for assessing changing landscape character of cultural landscapes in Flanders (Belgium). *Land Use Policy.* 26(4), 901-910.

Vecco, M. (2010). A definition of cultural heritage: From the tangible to the intangible. *Journal of Cultural Heritage.* 11(3), 321-324.

Vejre, H., Jensen, F. S. and Thorsen, B. J. (2010). Demonstrating the importance of intangible ecosystem services from peri-urban landscapes. *Ecological complexity.* 7(3), 338-348.

Velarde, M. D., Fry, G. and Tveit, M. (2007). Health effects of viewing landscapes–Landscape types in environmental psychology. *Urban Forestry & Urban Greening.* 6(4), 199-212.

WHC. (1994). *Convention Concerning the Protection of the World Cultural and Natural Heritage: World Heritage Committee, Seventh Session, Cartagena, Colombia, 6-11 December 1993: Report.* UNESCO.

Wheeler, A. (2014). Cultural Diplomacy, Language Planning, and the Case of the University of Nairobi Confucius Institute. *Journal of Asian and African Studies.* 49(1), 49-63.

Woodside, A. G., Hsu, S.-Y. and Marshall, R. (2011). General theory of cultures' consequences on international tourism behavior. *Journal of Business Research.* 64(8), 785-799.

Yisa, S. A. (2013). Nupe heritage dictionary (English-Nupe) Egan 'yekpe Nupe. In Yisa, S. A. (Ed.), (pp. 713). Minna Niger State Nigeria: Kochita resources limited.

Zhang, X., Zhou, L., Wu, Y., Skitmore, M. and Deng, Z. (2015). Resolving the conflicts of sustainable world heritage landscapes in cities: Fully open or limited access for visitors? *Habitat International.* 46, 91-100.

Zube, E. H. and Pitt, D. G. (1981). Cross-cultural perceptions of scenic and heritage landscapes. *Landscape Planning.* 8(1), 69-87.

Glossary

Asali	-	Place of origin and also used as being indigenous
Chigbe	-	Medicinal Herb, remedy and medications mostly from tree roots, leaves and barks
Dangi	-	Kin and blood relations
Dango	-	Soft grass used for reinforcing the mixture of mud in construction
Dazhi	-	The name of the village head of Doko and also the name of a clan in whose lineage have been leading the community.
Dende	-	The native name for the telecommunication mast found on the hill which was installed by the British engineers during colonial rule.
Dzoro	-	Collective and also a cooperative farm work organized on a rotational basis within a given age group of friends
Dzuko	-	Market space and also commercial transactions
Dzungi	-	Small private side entrance into the compounds and also a link from one courtyard to another
Edo	-	The granary mostly built of mud and used for the storage of grains
Edoko	-	Old name of Doko
Efako	-	A family system of the Nupe community which is based on the collective work on a large parcel of land for the collective good of the family. Members of this family could also be non-biological and all have equal rights social transactions
Efo	-	This has various uses which include its use to mean time and period in relation to events
Ega	-	A mud pen usually built of mud to house chickens, goats, and pigeons, they are usually located within the compounds
Egba	-	The name of the master mansion

Egbangi	-	Named from *egban* (congregation space)
Egbe	-	The calling of associations and relationship of group to collectively work on a project. It usually involves physical labour such as clearing of the roads, farm projects for the community or even the village head
Eguko	-	A place of convergence for ritual
Ejegi	-	Name of a stream
Eka	-	Multiple contextual uses to mean season or period
Emi	-	Home
Emitso	-	Literally, means the owner of the house, but mostly refer to the leadership of the compound
Enunu	-	Farming
Etsu dzuko	-	The market chief as well as leader
Ewon	-	A large depression of land that gets flooded annually and used for fishing
Eya	-	It means age and also a year
Gbagbako	-	Manually plowed ridge of 30-60cm thick made across as embankments at the rice farm to control the level of water.
Gbanchi	-	A fig tree, of which there are two species found in the Nupe community (*Ficus platyphylla*) grown to provide shade in compounds
Gbara	-	Manually ploughed ridge of about 15-20cm thick
Gbigba	-	It means praise, reverence, glorification and worship
Gozan	-	A name given to the person whom collectively offer multiple services of haircut, native medicine, circumcisions, manicure, and tattooing
Gunnu	-	An old Nupe traditional religious practice which involves rituals of anti-witchcraft, anti-crime, and also fertility of the women.
Kata	-	Bedroom
Katagi	-	Literally means a small room for cooking, kitchen
Katamba	-	An entrance hall builds original of circular form, it serves as an entrance and also a place for receiving guests

Kin	-	Motherland or region
Kintsozh	-	The upland Nupe people
Konufu	-	The name of a compound whose profession is mainly of *gozan.*
Kukpe	-	A system of building of mud wall in which the base is made thick of about 600mm and thins out as it reaches the roofing level to about 300mm
Kuti	-	God, idol, cult, masquerade, oracle and also communication with the deity
Kyadya	-	The riverine Nupe man and also the canoe man
Lati yan efo	-	The period of farm activity from sunrise to afternoon last for about 6 hours (10 am to 4 pm)
Lozungi	-	The period of farm activity from in the evening two hours before sunset (4 pm to 6 pm)
Manfu	-	The Islamic cleric's house
Nanche	-	A cooking spot mostly open and within the courtyard. It is made of three large stones in which fuel wood is utilised for cooking
Ndamitso	-	The owner of the compound which also means the head of the compound
Ndasonkyra	-	The title of the person elected to head a group who serve as a comforter of misfortune or tragedy in the community.
Pafi	-	A system of building mud walls in which dried mud blocks are laid one after the other using wet mud as the binder
Pati	-	The hill surrounding the Doko community which also served as the first place of settlement
Sakafugi	-	A period of going to the farm before the break of dawn to the rise of the sun, it takes about two hours of work.
Shegi	-	A mat made of reed grass which serves as a blind for the doorway
Shikpata	-	Toilet
Takogi	-	A section of the village located down the valley

Toro	-	A ditch excavated on a mud quarry, which is continually filled with water during the dry seasons to soften the surrounding mud for easy digging
Tsoede	-	The cultural hero of the Nupe people, who was born in ca 1500 and refer to as the founder of the Nupe kingdom
Tswata	-	The name of a compound whose profession is Blacksmithing
Wasa	-	Anti-snake portion which is placed in little sacks or suitable containers around the premises to protect such places from dangerous reptile. It is also used as an anti-dote of snake bites and sometimes used also as an antidote for witchcrafts. It is also a ritual associated with the performance of the anti-snake portion
Wuru	-	Shade
Yekun	-	A cylindrically shaped oven built to a height of about 1200mm and a diameter of 900mm split in the middle with a sieve-like decking used for quicker drying of grains during the raining season.
Zaman	-	Period
Zhempa,	-	A courtyard
Zhitsu	-	Old name for the village head of the community

Index

www.ingramcontent.com/pod-product-compliance
Lightning Source LLC
Chambersburg PA
CBHW072147020426
42334CB00018B/1911